Charles Cuthbert Hall

The Gospel of the Divine Sacrifice

A Study in Evangelical Belief with Some Conclusions Touching Life

Charles Cuthbert Hall

The Gospel of the Divine Sacrifice
A Study in Evangelical Belief with Some Conclusions Touching Life

ISBN/EAN: 9783337165697

Printed in Europe, USA, Canada, Australia, Japan

Cover: Foto ©Lupo / pixelio.de

More available books at **www.hansebooks.com**

THE GOSPEL

OF THE

DIVINE SACRIFICE

A Study in Evangelical Belief

WITH SOME CONCLUSIONS TOUCHING LIFE

BY

CHARLES CUTHBERT HALL, D.D.

MINISTER OF THE FIRST PRESBYTERIAN CHURCH OF BROOKLYN
NEW YORK

NEW YORK
DODD, MEAD AND COMPANY
1897

TO

The Memory of My Father

A THOUGHTFUL BELIEVER IN THE SAVIOUR, WHOM HE
NOW BEHOLDS

THESE PAGES ARE INSCRIBED

WITH FILIAL APPRECIATION, GRATITUDE, AND
AFFECTION

CONTENTS

CHAPTER		PAGE
I.	THE ATONEMENT NOT THE CAUSE OF GOD'S LOVE, BUT LOVE THE CAUSE OF THE ATONEMENT	3
II.	THE EXTENT OF THE ATONEMENT; OR, FOR WHOM DID CHRIST DIE?	29
III.	WHY NOT FORGIVENESS WITHOUT SACRIFICE?	57
IV.	THE SORROW OF CHRIST IN HIS SACRIFICE	87
V.	THE JOY OF CHRIST IN HIS SACRIFICE	119
VI.	THE REJECTION OF THE ATONEMENT	149
VII.	THE PROBLEM OF HUMAN SUFFERING CONSIDERED IN THE LIGHT OF THE DIVINE SACRIFICE	179
VIII.	THE SOVEREIGNTY OF GOD	209
IX.	THE APPLICATION OF THE SACRIFICE OF CHRIST TO THE PRESENT CONDITION OF SOCIETY	237

Contents

CHAPTER PAGE
X. THE NEW TESTAMENT IDEA OF HUMAN
PERSONALITY 267
XI. CONDUCT; OR, THE CROWNING OF
ONESELF 293

Introductory Note

THE following pages represent the attempt of an individual to state for himself the meaning of the Divine Sacrifice. The historic Confessions of the Protestant Church are not meant to deter the individual from making his own studies in New Testament truth. They are meant rather to stimulate inquiry, and to encourage first-hand use of the Scriptures. True reverence for those Confessions, and grateful appreciation of their value, may coexist with humble efforts to think out for oneself "the mystery which hath been hid from ages and from generations, but now is made manifest."

The writer disclaims all controversial intent in that which he has written. His aim has been to state, in terms of modern thought, "the glorious Gospel of the Blessed God;" to emphasize the bearing

Introductory Note

of the Atonement upon personality and upon conduct; to commend the Evangelical position to some thoughtful men and women who may have experienced difficulty in appropriating the supreme message of Christianity. The joy of life and the dignity of conduct are bound up in that supreme message of Christianity. There is, therefore, a place for any word, however crudely spoken, that may make Christ and His Sacrifice more intelligible to a human soul.

This book rests on three assumptions: The Authenticity of the Scriptures, the Inspiration of the Scriptures, the Godhead of Christ. These assumptions are logical in the premises. The writer could, if required, state the processes through which he has reached for himself thorough convictions of the Authenticity and Inspiration of the Holy Scriptures and of the Godhead of Jesus Christ. But this would be to extend the contents of the present work beyond proper limits. It is not necessary. The ultimate evidential test of the message of Christianity is in itself.

Introductory Note

The Gospel of the Divine Sacrifice is its own *Apologia*. In the breadth of its conception of God; in the axiomatic truth of its delineation of man; in the seraphic purity of its principles; in the regal majesty of its commandments; in the idyllic tenderness of its consolations, — the Gospel of the Cross demonstrates itself, to whomsoever will receive it, as the wisdom of God and the power of God unto salvation.

SINTON, WESTPORT,
August, A.D. 1896.

I

THE ATONEMENT NOT THE CAUSE OF GOD'S LOVE, BUT LOVE THE CAUSE OF THE ATONEMENT

We have seen and do testify, that the Father sent the Son to be the Saviour of the world.

First Epistle of St. John.

But God commendeth His own love toward us, in that while we were yet sinners, Christ died for us. Much more then, being now justified by His blood, shall we be saved from the wrath of God through Him.

Epistle to the Romans.

Chapter I

The Atonement not the Cause of God's Love, but Love the Cause of the Atonement

CHRISTIANITY is the Gospel of the Divine Sacrifice. Christianity derives its name from Christ, its meaning from the Cross. Reduced to its simplest terms Christianity gives Jesus Christ and Him crucified. This, the essence of Christianity, forms the subject of the following pages. The conditions of our time invite the study of this subject. Our time is a crowded, pushing, keen-witted time; there are many gospels, — gospels of ambition, gospels of selfishness, gospels of progress, gospels of worldly and churchly pride. It is a time of all times to consider the

Gospel of the Divine Sacrifice. The conditions of our lives invite the study of this subject. Those who are trained to think for themselves, not to do their thinking by proxy, are also tempted to think too little about Jesus Christ and Him crucified. It becomes easier to accept the forms of Christianity than to realize its essence; that which is spiritual tends to sink into that which is habitual; the vision of God to fade into the light of common day. The glory of God calls for the study of this subject. "God, Who at sundry times and in divers manners spake in time past unto the fathers by the prophets, hath in these last days spoken unto us by His Son." The Gospel of the Divine Sacrifice is God's message by His Son. Christ is the Word,—the Message Incarnate,— Him we must hear. "See," said one of old, "that ye refuse not Him That speaketh.

The Atonement

For if they escaped not, when they refused Him That warned them on earth, much more shall not we escape who turn away from Him That warneth from heaven: Whose voice then shook the earth: but now hath He promised, saying: Yet once more will I make to tremble, not the earth only, but also the heaven."

The present observations on this subject proceed from an attempt (begun long since in the writer's own private studies of the Word, and for the sake of satisfying the hunger of his own heart, and continued in the larger hope of helping others), to find a starting-point from which to think one's way into the Gospel of the Divine Sacrifice; into the truth "Jesus Christ and Him crucified;" into the essence of Christianity. The result of this attempt has been the evolution of a formula: The Atonement not the cause of God's Love, but Love the cause of the Atonement. This formula furnishes a convenient starting-point from which to begin to think one's way into the problem of "Jesus Christ and Him crucified." There must be a starting-point from which the human mind shall begin its study of the Divine Sacrifice. Intellectually, a starting-point is a necessity. The proposition, "Jesus Christ and Him crucified" is too great to be taken up as an incident, a detached event, to be considered by itself. There must be something back of it, something prior to it, some antecedent fact of some kind, of which fact "Jesus Christ and Him crucified" is the result. The question then is: What is that antecedent fact upon which the mind may rest, and from which the mind may begin, as from a starting-point, to work its way up to the supreme consummation, which is the Divine Sacrifice? Spiritually, a starting-point is a necessity. If the Holy

The Atonement

Spirit reveals to us a Saviour Whom we are to worship, He must, in order that we may worship Him intelligently, also reveal the cause of which the Saviour's work is the result. Faith requires a starting-point from which to pursue its course, a fundamental idea on which to build, an underlying ultimate cause, in which, as in the socket of Calvary's rock, to plant the Cross. Deny this to faith, and faith in Jesus Christ and Him crucified becomes a vague and fitful conception, floating about a cross which is rather a figure of speech than a fixed and unalterable reality. The soul hungers to find that starting-point. It cannot take Jesus Christ and Him crucified as an incident, an after-thought, an heroic rescue devised in an emergency. It feels instinctively that the Cross must be the result of some deeper cause. It demands to be led to that deeper cause, that it may make it the starting-point of thought. Such a starting-point is provided in the formula: The Atonement not the cause of God's Love, but Love the cause of the Atonement. In defining this formula it becomes necessary to state the assumptions on which it rests. They are three in number: the authenticity of the Scriptures, the inspiration of the Scriptures, the Godhead of Christ. It is not essential, for our present purpose, to sketch even in outline the process of thought by which an unprejudiced mind may be satisfied of the authenticity of the Scriptures, of the inspiration of the Scriptures, and of the Godhead of Jesus Christ; it is sufficient to announce that these three propositions are assumed as the basis of all that may hereafter be said.

It will be observed that the formula contains two declarations, — one negative, one positive.

I. The negative declaration: The

The Atonement

Atonement is not the cause of God's Love. When one who desires a settled faith in the Atonement, and who feels that the Death of Christ must be more than a mere tragic incident in history, begins to search for that ultimate idea which lies beneath the Atonement, and which explains it, he may think he has found it in the idea of a loving Saviour interposing to shield guilty sinners from an angry God. As he turns the pages of his Bible, his eyes fall on many passages which speak of the wrath of God, and of the punishment of sin; and then in melting contrast to those fearful passages breathing of judgment, the face of Christ shines upon him from the same Bible, — the face of the Man of Sorrows, pale with fatigue, seamed with grief, scarred with the wounds from a thorny crown, marvellous in pity, compassion, willingness to suffer. As these two opposite ideas meet him

The Atonement

again and again in his study of the Bible,— the wrath of God, the tenderness and self-sacrifice of Jesus,— he feels the force of the contrast between them working out a practical result in his own thought. God is contrasted with Christ. God the stern and terrible punisher of sin; Christ the meek and gentle lamb; Christ the voluntary offering, placing himself between the terrible wrath of God and the defenceless head of man, and receiving upon Himself the storm of wrath. And as his thought crystallizes around these two contrasted ideas, he conceives of God as a Being Whose wrath has been appeased by the Atonement, Who loves us because Christ has died for us; and thus the ultimate idea lying back of the Atonement appears to be that the Atonement is the cause of God's love. Christ is thus represented to the mind as having in His love and compassion stepped between man and

The Atonement

God to make God feel differently toward man, to make Him love man, Who but for Christ would not have loved man. It is easy for any one familiar with the New Testament to see how this contrast between the wrath of God and the love of Christ, or, to speak more exactly, this contrast between God and Christ can be supported by texts of Scripture, and nothing could be farther from the writer's purpose than to criticise or to condemn the opinions of those who are persuaded that this is the deepest idea beneath the Atonement: that the Atonement is the cause of God's love, that God loves man because of the Atonement, because Christ died. But as one studies the effects of this view in the spiritual life of people, one sees certain things which suggest the thought that this may not be the ultimate idea which underlies the great truth of Jesus Christ and Him crucified. For the effect of this view seems to be the introduction of discord into the Holy Trinity, setting the Father against the Son, and the Son against the Father in Their respective attitudes toward man. The Father is stern and wrathful; the Son is tender and pitiful; the Father has lifted His hand to strike and destroy; the Son, moved by a holy passion to save, has flung Himself into the very path of descending judgment, to receive its shock upon His own Person. Can this be our deepest and best thought of God? Can this thought lead us as far as we may be led into the conception of the perfect unity of life and purpose which exists in the Triune Godhead? Moreover, as one traces the results of this proposition, that the love of God is caused by Christ's Atonement, as these results work themselves out in many of the lives brought in contact with the idea, one feels that in reaching this idea we have not gone so far as we may

The Atonement

go to find a starting-point for our thought of the Atonement. For one encounters two opposite results which apparently develop from the proposition that the Atonement is the cause of love. One result is a form of clinging to Christ which practically separates Him from God. We find one trusting, loving, clinging to, confiding in Jesus as a shelter from God; much as a child runs to its mother and buries its face in her arms to shut out from view some gloomy figure that has terrified it. The other result is substantially the rejection of the Atonement as something unworthy of God; the setting aside of Jesus as Mediator, from the feeling that God is too great, too noble, too good to demand the blood of an innocent victim such as Christ was, before He will be induced to love man. There are those who deny the Atonement out of respect for God; they feel unwilling to attribute to God a nature

The Atonement

so revengeful that He will not love man until He has seen His own Son stretched in deadly anguish and ignominy on the Cross.

II. Observing for years these results working themselves out respectively in various classes of minds (while, one is also bound to say, many others seem to experience no diffculty in holding that the Atonement is the cause of God's love), it has appeared to the writer possible to reach some still deeper basis of thought where one might establish a starting-point whence to think one's way on to Jesus Christ and Him crucified. And in this formula, the positive proposition of which is now presented, that deeper basis of thought is humbly suggested. It is this: The Atonement not the cause of God's Love, but Love the cause of the Atonement. Not this: God loves us because Christ died for us; but this: Because God loves us

The Atonement

Christ died for us. Love the cause of the Atonement. "We have seen and do testify, that the Father sent the Son to be the Saviour of the world." "God commendeth His own love toward us, in that while we were yet sinners, Christ died for us."

As one takes the Bible into one's hand, and with an open mind and a prayerful spirit brings together all the material in it bearing upon the formula now before us; doing this in absolute honesty, neither suppressing any fact in the interest of a theory, nor buttressing any preconceived opinion by an artful use of Scripture, — four thoughts present themselves, and form in their relation to one another a starting-point from which to think our way up to Jesus Christ and Him crucified: The Unity of God. What Man is to God. What Sin is to God. What Atonement is to God.

1. The Unity of God. Not alone

on the quotation of simple and separate texts rests this most fundamental conception of our religion. It is involved philosophically and ethically in the Christian concept of God. There is One God, and if in His mysterious love He reveals Himself to us as Three in One, the very terms of that revelation preclude the thought of conflicting purpose or contrasted feelings in the life of the Godhead. The thought of the Father hating while the Son is loving; of the Father destroying while the Son is saving, becomes unthinkable when we stand within the precinct of the Word. Explicitly have we been told of that eternal Unity. Christ declared it: "The Comforter will not speak from Himself, but what He shall hear, that shall He speak." "The Son can do nothing of Himself, but what He seeth the Father do." "The Father is glorified in the

The Atonement

Son." If we behold in the Father holy wrath against sin, we may know that the Son, gentle and gracious though He be, shares in all its fulness that passion of holy wrath. If we behold in the Son tenderness and grace, the spirit of self-giving for the sake of man, we may know, whatever else we seem to see in God, that that marvellous, sacrificial love for humanity is also in the heart of the Father. "He that hath seen me," said Christ, "hath seen the Father."

2. What Man is to God. Because we have in the Bible declarations of the wrath of God, and demonstrations of the judgment of God, some have concluded that the attitude of God's heart toward man is that of revengeful passion, which has simply been appeased by the shedding of Christ's blood; and that the love which is now predicated of God is not a love for us, so to speak, in our own right, but a love for

The Atonement

Christ the Son, the benefit of which only indirectly comes to us. But not to this conclusion is one necessarily led in one's study of God as related to man. If any one would know what man is to God, let him study that relationship as it appeared before sin entered the world to darken the scene; let him look upon man as he stood before God in the simplicity of an unfallen state, beautiful, stainless, glorious, a child worthy of his Father. And what then was man to God in the unfallen state? He was God's child, and God was his Father, and God's delight was in him, and God's hopes were centered upon him, and God's world was given him for a home, and God's banner over him was love. What man was to God then, when he had not sinned, but when God knew that man's personal freedom made it possible for him to sin, that man is to God to-day, when he has sinned, and come short of the

The Atonement

glory of God, and has brought down on him the wrath of God, and done things worthy of death Man was dear to God then in the sinless state. He is dear to God now in that sinful state which inevitably exposes him to the wrath of holiness. Man has changed; God has not changed. God loved him then, God loves him now. God was his Father then, God is his Father now. The calm study of the Scriptures appears to justify not only, but to require, a belief in the Fatherhood of God toward all men, — the saintliest and the most devil-possessed. This is the thought from which some shrink because of the rash conclusion which has been drawn from it. The Fatherhood of God is sometimes represented as in itself an all-sufficient relationship, which renders the Atonement unnecessary, and which sinks the penal consequences of sin in an unfathomable ocean of Divine benevolence. Men rashly talk of the Fatherhood of God as if it were a universal indulgence, a license to sin. And for this reason some with much cause shrink from using the term lest it be made a snare. But it is not necessary, it is not practicable, to surrender a term which, however it may have been perverted, contains the essential thought of Christianity, — that man is dear to God, that God loves man as the offspring of His own life; and that all that has been done for man's redemption springs from the eternal love in the heart of God which would not let man go into self-destruction without placing an Atonement within his reach.

3. *What Sin is to God.* It is in realizing this that we have most signally failed, and in failing here we have failed to realize the true intensity of those blended passions — the passion of wrath and the passion of love — that meet in the

The Atonement

Atonement. Who can realize what sin is to God: how horrible an offence to His nature; how gross an intrusion upon the order of His universe; how intolerable a condition which must be beaten down and stamped out with the vengeance of righteousness? They who suppose that wrath against sin is incompatible with God's Fatherhood show by that supposition that they have failed to grasp the essential conditions of life as they exist in a holy Being. We have not understood what God is until we are able to speak of the wrath of holy love against sin. If God is love, and God is holy, the wrath of holy love, august, terrible, pure, is the necessary condition of such a Being in the presence of sin. There is a wrath known on earth which is born of sinfulness, and is filled with hatred. Such wrath is of the devil, a hellish passion. But the wrath of God is the wrath of holy love,

The Atonement

the protest of God's truth and beauty and purity and love against that which, by disorganizing the universe, obstructs His purpose of eternal affection toward a race made in His own Image, born out of His own life. Ah, what is sin to God! If we in moments of pure and noble thought have suddenly been stricken by it, and have felt the just wrath of righteousness rising up within us, what must be the wrath of God against the sin cherished in human lives; pursued and followed after by human passions; wrought out to the foul and bitter end in human histories!

4. What, then, is the Atonement to God? Ask that question in the light of these preceding thoughts, — what man is to God, and what sin is to God. Man is the dear object of God's love; sin is the intolerable outrage against God's nature, filling God's universe with

The Atonement

lawlessness and misery. Atonement is the supreme effort of God's love, by His own suffering to save man from that sin which makes him an object of God's wrath. Put side by side these two Scriptures: "The wrath of God is revealed from heaven against all ungodliness and unrighteousness of men," — that is the essential attitude of God's holiness towards sin; — " But God commendeth His own love toward us, in that, while we were yet sinners, Christ died for us; much more then, being now justified by His blood, we shall be saved from the wrath of God through Him."

We return, then, to the formula, believing it to express the spirit of the Scriptures: The Atonement not the cause of God's Love, but Love the cause of the Atonement. The Atonement is the expression on earth of a love that filled God's heart from the beginning. The Atone-

The Atonement

ment is God's self-giving to save us from the holy wrath under which our sins have brought us. The love of the holy God is the starting-point from which to think one's way up to Jesus Christ and Him crucified. Begin there, with the knowledge that God is love. Be sure that a holy God loves you. Be sure that because He is holy, His wrath, the indignant, sorrowful wrath of holy love, is revealed from heaven against all ungodliness and unrighteousness of men. Be sure that that tremendous love has expressed itself in sacrificial suffering to save you from that tremendous wrath. Take these thoughts, put them together, and realize two facts: the nature of sin, the Person of Christ. Realize the nature of sin; it is a scorn of the Atonement, a contempt of God's supreme declaration of love, a delivering over of one's self to wrath, the wrath which is, because God is holy. Realize the

The Atonement

Person of Christ. Behold in Him the holy God Whose wrath is revealed against sin, suffering in the flesh for love, to save from that wrath. Realize the Godhead of Christ. Grasp the sense in which Christ declares the Unity of Godhead when He says: "I and my Father are One;" and realizing the Unity of the Godhead, bow before the Cross as before a throne.

II

THE EXTENT OF THE ATONEMENT; OR, FOR WHOM DID CHRIST DIE?

Jesus Christ the righteous is the propitiation for our sins; and not for ours only, but also for the whole world.

First Epistle of St. John.

We behold Him Who hath been made a little lower than the angels, even Jesus, because of the suffering of death crowned with glory and honor, that by the grace of God He should taste death for every man.

Epistle to the Hebrews.

Chapter II

The Extent of the Atonement; or, For whom did Christ die?

THE subject now brought to our attention is the Extent of the Atonement. This is the next step, logically speaking, following the position defined in the preceding chapter. We sought a basis on which to rest the idea of an Atonement; a starting-point from which to think our way up to Jesus Christ and Him crucified. That basis we found in the proposition: The Atonement not the cause of God's Love, but Love the cause of the Atonement. Examining the former and negative member of the proposition in the light of Scripture, we concluded that the Atonement is

The Extent of the Atonement

not the cause of God's love, inasmuch as there could not be division and conflict of motives in the Godhead; the Father hating man and wishing to destroy him; the Son loving man and interposing to save him from the Father, and to turn the disposition of the Father from wrath to love. Examining the latter and positive member of the proposition, we concluded that "Jesus Christ and Him crucified" is the supreme expression of the love of the Father; that, in the words of St. John, "the Father sent the Son to be the Saviour of the world," and that in the words of St. Paul, "God commendeth His own love toward us, in that, while we were yet sinners, Christ died for us." And our starting-point was, accordingly, thus defined; not in the pride of reason, nor with the confidence of dogmatic assertion, but in the humility and reverence befitting those who are founding all their

The Extent of the Atonement

thought upon the authenticity of Scripture, the inspiration of Scripture, and the Godhead of Christ: *Not* God loves us because Christ died for us, but Christ died for us because God loves us.

With this starting-point ascertained and defined, the next step is to inquire into the extent of the Atonement; that is to say, the wideness of its application. Assuming the Atonement to be the supreme expression of God's love, the question follows: To whom is this expression of love addressed? On whose behalf did the Atonement take place? For whom did Christ die? For one? for some? or for all?

It is quite evident that both the degree of interest and the kind of interest excited in our minds by the Atonement are affected by our opinion of its extent. An event which concerns one, or some, cannot rank in interest with an event which

The Extent of the Atonement

equally concerns all. All men of intelligence may take a certain kind of interest in an occurrence affecting one individual, or one class of individuals; but the interest so awakened is different in kind as well as in degree from that which every man takes in an event immediately affecting himself.

In the foregoing observations on the subject of the Atonement, and in all that may follow, the writer desires only that he may be regarded as a seeker after truth in the Word of God. He has no discoveries to announce, no original conclusions to propound, no claim to make upon public attention which rests in intellectual certitude; above all, no assault to bring against those whose thought has worked out on other lines. He is but a seeker after truth in the place where alone the truth he seeks may be found, — that is, in the inspired Scriptures. Other truths may be sought and

The Extent of the Atonement

found in other places. Astronomy has its own gospel of the glory of God to proclaim from the star spaces of the ecliptic and the orbits of the planets; Archæology has its own gospel of the antiquity of man to proclaim from the lake-dwellings of Switzerland, the shell-mounds of Denmark, the caves of Belgium and Sicily and Gibraltar; but the Gospel of the Divine Sacrifice is proclaimed only from the Scriptures, and apart from them we have no means of comprehending the work of Christ. It is, however, impossible to give any answer whatsoever to the question " For whom did Christ die ? " without referring to the great historical divide which distinguishes those who interpret the Scripture teaching on the death of Christ as declaring a limited Atonement from those who interpret that teaching as the declaration of a universal Atonement. There are four ways of answering the question, " For

The Extent of the Atonement

whom did Christ die?" He died for none; or He died for some one favored individual; or He died for a portion of the human race; or He died for all.

With the first and the second of these answers we have no concern, as the facts of Scripture sweep them aside. It cannot be that Christ died for no one, that His death was a mere catastrophe resulting from His own determination to oppose and rebuke the Jews; for the Word of God represents His death as containing a purpose and a result intended to affect life other than His own. It cannot be that Christ died in the heroism of personal self-devotion for some one favored individual between whom and death he thrust Himself, as the victim of an intrepid friendship; for all the facts of the case are known to us without the suggestion of any person on whose individual behalf He laid down His life. There remain open, therefore, only these alterna-

The Extent of the Atonement

tives, — he died for some, or he died for all: a limited Atonement or a universal Atonement.

The distinction between these two modes of interpreting the Scriptures we may describe as the great divide in distinctively Christian thought. It would take a volume to give merely the literary and ecclesiastical history of the great divide, and to follow through their infinitely interesting modifications and progressions the movements of thought on either side of this vast question: " For whom did Jesus Christ lay down His life?" To a thoughtful and clear-visioned mind these movements are infinitely interesting. Such minds will not turn impatiently from the intense and anxious reasonings with which those who lived before us pondered the Cross and sought to read aright its message to mankind. Nor will such minds disparage the controversial literature on the Atonement as but

The Extent of the Atonement

the cobweb-weaving and the hair-splitting of men who had become the devotees of speculative theology. For one finds in the times in which we live, and among the men and women whom we touch, the same anxious reasonings around the Cross; the same longing to obtain in the Word of God some answer to the question " For whom did Christ die ? " which will meet and satisfy all other scriptural statements bearing on the destiny of man under the government of God. The great divide exists to-day, and on the one side or on the other side each individual mind tends to find an answer which may for itself best satisfy the conditions of the case. Is it a limited Atonement? or is it a universal Atonement? Did He die for some? or did He die for all?

To those who have not thought their way down into the depths of this subject, and who have not carefully searched their Bibles and

The Extent of the Atonement

brought together all that they contain, not only respecting the Death of Christ, but also respecting the destiny of man; to those who have lived merely upon the broad surface of the general idea that Christ died for mankind, — it may appear a most unaccountable and uncalled for circumstance that any question should ever have arisen on the extent of the Atonement; that any one ever supposed the Atonement to be limited in its extent; that all persons have not agreed and taken for granted that the Atonement is universal, and that Christ died for all. And this surprise that any have hesitated to affirm a universal Atonement deepens into curiosity under the statement that from a very early period in the history of Christian thought it has seemed impossible and unscriptural to multitudes of intelligent and devout persons to affirm, in plain, unguarded words, that Christ died

The Extent of the Atonement

for the whole world. Curiosity concentrates itself upon the reason why this is so, — why any one should raise the question of extent, or conceive the idea of a limited Atonement. What suggests the thought that the Atonement is not for all? An answer should be given to satisfy this entirely proper curiosity. It may be given in one sentence: The conception of a limited Atonement arises from a certain mode of stating the doctrine of Election. It may be said with some degree of probability that no believer in the New Testament might ever have thought of saying that Christ did not die for all, except for a certain interpretation which was placed, very early in the history of Christian thought, upon those scriptures of the New Testament which speak of God's election and predestination of men. For, leaving for the moment out of view the scriptures speaking of Election, the natu-

The Extent of the Atonement

ral meaning of those which speak of the extent of the Atonement would plainly appear to be that Christ died for all. The natural meaning, for example, of the following verses would appear to be, apart from any theory to the contrary, that Jesus Christ laid down His life for the whole human race, without limit or distinction of persons. " Jesus Christ the Righteous is the propitiation for our sins, and not for ours only, but also for the whole world." " We behold Him Who hath been made a little lower than the angels, even Jesus, because of the suffering of death crowned with glory and honor, that by the grace of God He should taste death for every man." If one who had never read a line of dogmatic theology were to pick up a slip of paper bearing these words, it is probable that they would suggest to his mind an Atonement for the race, not an atonement for a portion of the

The Extent of the Atonement

race only. But all who have read the Epistle to the Romans, more especially the ninth chapter of that epistle, and other great passages bearing on the same line, are aware that the New Testament teaches God's election of men quite as certainly as it teaches God's redemption of the world through Christ. But what, one asks, have these Election scriptures to do with a limited Atonement? They have everything to do with a limited Atonement if one places upon them the interpretation which, from early times down to this time, has been placed upon them by large numbers of intelligent and devout persons. Under that interpretation they become the cause from which springs the fair and necessary conclusion that the Lord Jesus Christ died not for all men, but only for some men. Under that interpretation they become the barrier to prevent one from logically holding any

The Extent of the Atonement

other conclusion than that Christ did not, in a real sense, die for all. The interpretation of the Election scriptures to which we refer is that which regards the decree of God as unconditional. By the unconditional decree is meant that God eternally chose or elected a certain portion of the race unto necessary and everlasting life and blessedness, and that the remainder of the human race, being not included in the scope of that eternal decree, is necessarily and everlastingly excluded from the life and blessedness contemplated in the decree. This decree is said to be unconditional, in that they who are in it cannot fall out of it; they who are out of it cannot come into it. But what connection has this interpretation of the Election scriptures with the Extent of our Lord's Atonement? A vital connection. For under this interpretation of the decree as unconditional, the Atonement is the

The Extent of the Atonement

step taken by God, not to redeem the entire fallen race, but to accomplish the salvation of that portion of the race which by this unconditional decree He has eternally elected unto necessary and everlasting life. In other words, Christ died for the unconditionally elected, and not for the whole world. Those who have accepted the logical conclusion that the Atonement is limited in its actual effect to the unconditionally elected, do also claim that in a sense the Atonement may be regarded as universal, inasmuch as the infinite value of the Divine Sacrifice would make it sufficient, potentially, for an infinite number of human souls; but the natural and plain sense of the words, " He died for all," is carefully modified and restricted by the statement that the benefit of our Lord's death cannot possibly be applied to any save to those who are included in the decree of unconditional election.

The Extent of the Atonement

Clear statements of this position may be found in the writings of Dr. Charles Hodge, as, for example, in the following words: "There is a sense in which Christ died for all men. He died sufficiently for all. It follows from the nature of the Covenant of Redemption, as presented in the Bible, that Christ did not die equally for all mankind, but that He gave Himself for His people, and for their redemption."[1] If one dissents from this conclusion, it follows not that he dissents from the Election scriptures, nor that he does not consider them quite so truly a part of God's message to the world as the texts announcing a universal Atonement, to which reference has already been made. The Election scriptures need present no stumbling-block to the mind in its desire to believe a universal Atonement. One may accept them as reverently

[1] Systematic Theology, vol. ii. pp. 547, 560.

The Extent of the Atonement

and as gladly as one accepts the fourteenth chapter of St. John, or the twelfth chapter of Hebrews. Every fair and open mind will discriminate between dissent from anything in the Word of God, and dissent from certain interpretations which by men have been connected with certain portions of that Word, and have been regarded as authoritative and necessary interpretations. If the Election scriptures can only be understood to teach an unconditional decree, eternally electing some, eternally reprobating others, who are respectively elected or reprobated, not for anything in themselves, but alone at the sovereign pleasure of the Most High, then it is not easy to see a logical escape from the doctrine of an Atonement limited to the elect; in fact, some may prefer, under those circumstances, to believe the limited Atonement, inasmuch as the very words "Universal Atonement" would

The Extent of the Atonement

seem to mock at the misery of the non-elect. But one may be allowed to hope that the interpretation just described is not the only possible interpretation of the Election scriptures in the New Testament in accord with the Scriptures themselves. One may study that which is revealed in the New Testament concerning the Decree of God, and find nothing that affirms the destiny of the members of the human race to be unconditionally determined by that decree. Undoubtedly one finds in the New Testament Election and Reprobation. But what is the nature of that Election? It is possible (and in full conformity with Scripture) to look upon it as that eternal plan of love which dwelt always in the bosom of the Father for man whom He loves; for man, who is the offspring of His own life. The Election is thus the ideal of God for man, that every member of this our race entering into the

The Extent of the Atonement

world should be in this world (then contemplated as a holy and unfallen world), an incarnate image of the eternal Son. This Election one finds in the New Testament; the Father's eternal choice for us, the Father's predestination of us (in the counsel and plan of His own heart), that we should be a Christ-like race, conformed to the image of His Son. When the primitive, newly created man stood in godlike splendor of holiness and happiness in a holy and happy world, then began to be realized in the race the Election of God; then man stood before God as God's child, and God was his Father, and God's delight was in him and God's hopes were centred upon him, and God's world was given him for a home, and God's banner over him was love. Then came the dread catastrophe of sin, of man's choice contrary to the will of God, the first great falling of the creature below

The Extent of the Atonement

the Election and choice of the Creator. Yet in that catastrophe, the beginning of human sin, there was a certain godlike dignity. Man's power to sin,—that is to say, man's power to choose against God or with God,—was the great inalienable birthright of liberty from Him Whose breath was the life of man's spirit. And that catastrophe, working itself out in the stupendous devastation of a sin-stricken race, has never moved the heart of God from its eternal choice, its supreme Election. The love that was given to the unfallen man in forms of fellowship, still pours itself out upon the fallen man in the form of Atonement; and the Election of the Godhead, an election of glory and love, was manifested a second time as in a new creation, when, in the fulness of time, God sent forth His Son, born of a woman, born under the law, to redeem them that are under the law; that we, a race of sons who had thrown away our sonship, might in Christ receive the adoption of sons; and, because we are sons, God sent forth the spirit of His Son into our hearts, crying, " Abba, Father," declaring in our self-willed, stubborn hearts, the eternal choice of the Father for His children, that we should be conformed unto the image of His Son. This is thought to be a scriptural interpretation of the Election declared in the New Testament; an eternal plan for the race, conceived in the Father's heart, not turned aside by sin, but announced once more to the race in the Gospel of the Divine Sacrifice, and made possible once more to the race in Jesus the Righteous, Who is the propitiation for our sins, and not for ours only, but also for the whole world. If this be the Election, what is the Reprobation? If this be the revelation of "the riches of His glory upon vessels of mercy which He

The Extent of the Atonement

afore prepared unto glory," what is His reprobation of "vessels of wrath fitted to destruction?" It is the right of a holy God to reject vessels that refuse to be conformed to His purpose. One may speak of the wrath of God against sin, — the wrath of holy love, in the same breath with which one speaks of universal Atonement.

Some say: You must not say universal Atonement, for it implies universal salvation. Would to God it did certainly imply universal salvation! Would to God it were certainly true that as Christ tasted death for every man, every man shall taste life through Christ! Would to God there were no reason to believe that one soul for which Christ died shall be reprobate, a vessel of wrath fitted to destruction; reprobate before the face of God, not because the love that redeemed it is taken away, not because the

The Extent of the Atonement

Election of God towards it is other than a desire for its greatness and glory and peace, but because the soul, hardened through the deceitfulness of sin, glorying in its shame, plunging into darkness away from Light, persists unto the bitter end in treading under foot the Son of God, and in counting the Blood of the Covenant, wherewith it was sanctified, an unholy thing!

There are some conclusions which follow from a belief that the Atonement is universal, and that Christ tasted death for every man.

a. The Universal Influence of Sin and Death. "By one man sin entered into the world, and death by sin, and death passed upon all men, for that all have sinned." "He tasted death for every man." A universal condition called for a universal Atonement. What one needed, all needed. This is the great leveller of human distinctions. This is the common

The Extent of the Atonement

ground on which all men must meet. Why should one boast himself above another? Why should one scornfully condemn another? Are we not all resting in the one hope that Christ died for us? Are we not all needing the same Atonement? Let a man then lay off his pride, and be gentle before men and humble before God.

b. The Universal Obligation to live unto Him. "For the love of Christ constraineth us, because we thus judge that if one died for all, then were all dead, and that He died for all, that they which live should not henceforth live unto themselves, but unto Him Which died for them and rose again."

c. The Universal Importance and Value of Human Lives. "God so loved the world that He gave his only begotton Son." If God so loved it, what shall be our feeling toward it? What shall be our esti-

The Extent of the Atonement

mate and valuation of lives in the light of universal Atonement? "It is not the will of your heavenly Father that one of these little ones shall perish!" Can there be, then, a fellowship with God that is careless of man? a worship of God that is scornful of man? a love of God that does not include a broad reverence and holy compassion for human life as such, because of the Redemption?

d. The Universal Right of Lives to know the Gospel of their Redemption. When He Who redeemed the race had consummated that universal Atonement, He stood in His risen life upon the verge of His Ascension, and from His finished work He drew that last conclusion touching the right of a redeemed race to know of its Redemption:

"Thus it is written, that the Christ should suffer, and rise again the third day from the dead; and that repentance

The Extent of the Atonement

and remission of sins should be preached in His name unto all the nations. Ye are witnesses of these things."

"Go ye, therefore, and make disciples of all the nations, baptizing them into the name of the Father, and of the Son, and of the Holy Ghost, teaching them to observe all things whatsoever I commanded you: and lo, I am with you alway, even unto the end of the world."

III

WHY NOT FORGIVENESS WITHOUT SACRIFICE?

Knowing the judgment of God, that they which commit such things are worthy of death.
>> EPISTLE TO THE ROMANS.

And without shedding of blood is no remission.
>> EPISTLE TO THE HEBREWS.

For He hath made Him to be sin for us, Who knew no sin; that we might be made the righteousness of God in Him.
>> SECOND EPISTLE TO THE CORINTHIANS.

God, sending His own Son in the likeness of sinful flesh and as an offering for sin, condemned sin in the flesh: that the requirement of the law might be fulfilled in us, who walk not after the flesh, but after the spirit.
>> EPISTLE TO THE ROMANS.

Chapter III

Why not Forgiveness without Sacrifice?

IT is necessary now to consider a question which has troubled and unsettled many minds disposed to be fair and desiring to attain a definite faith. This question, raised at this point in the study of the Divine Sacrifice, appears to go back of conclusions already reached, and to disturb confidence in the validity of those conclusions.   It will be borne in mind that two conclusions have been reached in the foregoing chapters: first, that the love of God for man is the cause of the Atonement, which is the supreme expression of that love,— not that God loves us because Christ died for us, but that Christ died for us because God loves us; secondly, that the Atonement considered as to the extent of its reference to the human race is universal and unlimited; that Christ died for the whole world without distinction of persons, and not merely for a select portion of the race appointed unto an inevitable salvation by an unconditional decree. These are the two conclusions which have been reached, and to those who can accept them they are full of importance and of comfort. They present to the mind God standing in an attitude of love toward the whole race, contemplating the whole race with an eternal purpose and ideal of blessedness, and by means of Christ's Atonement creating a redeemed condition of the fallen race in which the attainment of the divine ideal is made at least a possibility for each member of that race. The effect of these conclusions upon some minds is to heighten immeasur-

Forgiveness without Sacrifice

ably their appreciation of the Atonement as an expression of the love of God.

But at this stage, when we are disposed to feel that we have found the true starting-point from which to think our way up to Jesus Christ and Him crucified, a question rises before us that tends, if it be not clearly and fully answered, to unsettle confidence in the validity of those conclusions which, prior to the arising of this question, appeared so reasonable, so satisfying, so scriptural, and so precious. This question is on the necessity of the Atonement. Why need there be any atonement? If God is love, as has been so positively affirmed, why should there be any atonement? Why is not forgiveness without sacrifice more worthy of God, and more credible in view of the alleged character of God, than forgiveness conditioned upon sacrifice, and upon the sacrifice of One Who is

Forgiveness without Sacrifice

innocent? This question is reasonable. It is not to be dismissed lightly or sternly, — lightly, as being a flippant and captious objection; sternly, as raising a doubt man has no right to raise. Man has a right to raise that doubt and to ask that question: "Why not forgiveness without sacrifice?" It is a question germane to the subject under discussion. It is a question of the utmost value and importance, because, from whatever motive it may be asked, whether from desire for instruction or from desire to assail the main position of evangelical religion, it furnishes an opportunity for the believer in the Atonement to disown some opinions erroneously attributed to him, and to state clearly and scripturally that which he does believe concerning the grounds on which the sacrifice of Christ may be regarded as a necessity.

The propriety, reasonableness, and force of this question: " Why not for-

Forgiveness without Sacrifice

giveness without sacrifice?" are seen when, by a process of analysis, we note the difference between this question and other doubts which are frequently raised against the Christian doctrine of the Atonement. This question, "Why not forgiveness without sacrifice?" is not a denial of sin as such. The sinfulness of sin is not disputed. Those who doubt the necessity of the Atonement may be in no doubt as to the moral distinction between good and evil. Some who have discarded the Atonement have been eminent in morality, keen in the discernment of right and wrong. Nor is this question a denial that sin calls for punishment. It assumes God's power to forgive sin, and that assumption implies as the antecedent of forgiveness God's right to punish sin. The right to punish is not denied. The justice of punishment as the proper judicial sequence of sin is not denied. The question is raised

Forgiveness without Sacrifice

on another issue, namely, whether God may not at His pleasure remit punishment by simple forgiveness without sacrifice. Nor is this question a denial that Christ died. It does not necessarily assail the historic data which point to Calvary. It does not decline to admit that such a Being as Jesus lived and labored in Palestine, and was condemned and crucified under Pontius Pilate. It does not refuse to join the unnumbered multitude of human minds grouped in veneration around the Cross. Admitting the death, it merely assigns to it a significance other than that of the Divine Sacrifice. Nor is this question a denial under all circumstances that Christ was competent to be in His death a sacrifice for sin. The denial of the Atonement may of course be the result of antecedent doubt concerning the divinity of Christ. But doubts concerning the Atonement may and do exist in

Forgiveness without Sacrifice

minds that have not called in question the divinity of Christ. Such doubts spring from a cause quite other than that of uncertainty as to the competency of Jesus to offer a sacrifice for the world. Such doubts call in question the propriety of the Atonement as an act of God. They raise the issue whether it is consistent with the glorious and perfect character of God to condition the forgiveness of man upon the sacrifice of the holy and beautiful Christ. This is a doubt of the Atonement inspired by reverence for God. By this process of analysis it must appear that the question, " Why not forgiveness without sacrifice?" is not flippant, improper, or essentially hostile to God, but serious, reasonable, and extremely important. If it were a question flippant or avowedly hostile to God, if it were a denial of sin, or a denial that sin calls for punishment, or a denial that Christ died, or a denial of

Forgiveness without Sacrifice

Christ's divinity, it could be dealt with fairly, of course, and kindly, of course, but with much less apprehensiveness of its power to unsettle evangelical belief. We could appeal to the instinct of human consciousness, to the facts of experience, to the annals of history, and thus sufficiently maintain our position. There are objections levelled against the Atonement which, like arrows shot against a granite cliff, shatter themselves without scarring the cliff. But this objection is not one of those. This may appeal to minds which luminously discern between good and evil, which admit the justice of punishment as the sequence of sin, which worship Christ's divinity. This touches a point antecedent to all conclusions upon the nature and extent of the Atonement. This inquires into the morality of a Being who could demand such a sacrifice as a condition precedent to the forgiveness of sin.

Forgiveness without Sacrifice

In the previous chapter upon the Extent of the Atonement, the opinion is expressed that no one would have thought of doubting that the Bible represents Christ as dying for the whole world, but for a certain interpretation which was connected with certain texts of the Bible very early in the history of Christian thought. The texts referring to God's election of men were interpreted to mean an unconditional decree, absolutely determining the destiny of individuals, whereby some were appointed unto an inevitable salvation, and others, not included in that decree, were negatively appointed unto an equally inevitable damnation. This interpretation of these texts was strongly pressed in the past, and was widely acquiesced in, as being the only right interpretation of the Election scriptures. As a result, the thought of a limited Atonement followed; that Christ died, not to redeem the entire race, but to secure the salvation of an elect portion of the race.

It has also been pointed out in a previous chapter that in the process of religious thought the teaching has been announced and has widely prevailed, that God the Father loves us because Christ died for us; that the anger of the Father was raised against man and was about to descend upon man, when the gentle, loving, and heroic Christ flung Himself between the stern Father and guilty man, received the outburst of wrath on His own innocent head, and that the Father, appeased by the blood of this self-sacrificing Victim, now consents to love us for the sake of Him Who became our champion and Who perished on our behalf. Thus there grew up in Christian thought the suggestion that the Christian Gospel distinguishes between the purpose of the Father and the purpose of the Son in dealing with the human race; that

Forgiveness without Sacrifice

the Father, being angry, wanted to destroy us for our sins, but the Son, being lovely, sympathetic, and heroically unselfish, interposed, and by a tragic self-surrender to the Father's wrath turned that wrath away. It is safe to say that this mode of stating the gospel,— a mode which would apparently imperil belief in the unity of the Godhead,— might never have become current if all whose duty it is to guide religious thought had kept themselves humbly and obediently close to the Bible, which announces in language no man need misunderstand: " We believe and do testify, that the Father sent the Son to be the Saviour of the world," and " God so loved the world that He gave His only begotten Son, that whosoever believeth in Him should not perish, but have everlasting life." It would be difficult to account for the extent to which the question, " Why not forgiveness without sacrifice ?"

Forgiveness without Sacrifice

has operated as a barrier to faith without referring, respectfully and with moderation, to the prominence once given in evangelistic teaching to the doctrine of the Unconditional Decree, and to the idea (incorporated alike in prose and in poetry) of the wrathful Father appeased by the merciful Son.

That the idea of an unconditional decree of Election adds force to the claim that forgiveness should take place without sacrifice will appear upon reflection. If it be true that the sovereign pleasure of God has decreed the inevitable salvation and blessedness of a portion of the race, appointing them thereto not because of any worthiness in themselves, but wholly as an exhibition of the right of sovereignty and the purpose of love, and if for the same august end of sovereignty the rest of the race, excluded from that decree, is doomed to an inevitable damnation, he who

Forgiveness without Sacrifice

claims forgiveness without sacrifice is inclined to ask why this situation should have its terrific simplicity disturbed by the introduction of Christ as an innocent and bloody sacrifice? On whose behalf, it is asked, could such a sacrifice be required? To whose advantage could it inure? Not to the damned, for they are damned not first of all in their own right and by their own misdeeds, but first of all by exclusion from an unconditional decree antedating their existence. And why, it is still further asked, should the elect require atonement if their election be the outcome of God's " mere free grace and love, without any foresight of faith or good works, or perseverance in either of them, or any other thing in the creature, as conditions or causes moving Him thereunto, and all to the praise of His glorious grace"? Why, it is asked (not by persons of flippant temper or hostile spirit, but

Forgiveness without Sacrifice

by those who seek a basis for their faith), if men are lost and saved on these grounds, is it not more merciful and consistent with God to spare the non-elect the torment of witnessing an atonement in whose efficacy they cannot share, and to spare Christ the misery of enduring supreme humiliation for those who, by a decree of election, were inevitably saved from all eternity? This is the inquiry of some minds that would fain be evangelical believers; and the rights of men seeking for a Biblical faith in Christ as a Saviour, justify the statement of their difficulty, and the respectful intimation of its possible cause.

It will also be seen that the idea, once so prevalent and so prominent, of the wrathful Father appeased by the merciful Son, may have operated to strengthen the claim that forgiveness without sacrifice is more credible, because more consonant with the

Forgiveness without Sacrifice

glorious and perfect character of God as a God of love than forgiveness conditioned on the sacrifice of the innocent. If Christian literature and Christian pulpits have represented God the Father as burning with a wrathful purpose to destroy man for his sins, and, being interrupted in that purpose by the intervention of the holy and compassionate Son, as seizing upon that spotless and uncomplaining victim and wreaking on him the vengeance which has its thirst slaked with Christ's blood,—the rejection of the Atonement by some persons of intelligence is not unlikely. Wherever this form of stating the Atonement gains ground, it tends to raise in some minds not hostile to God, but jealous rather to defend the glory and purity of God, some most disturbing and unsettling objections, all of which appear to strengthen the probability of forgiveness without sacrifice.

Forgiveness without Sacrifice

It is objected, to the idea of an angry Father's wrath being appeased by the blood of the innocent Son, that such an atonement, if offered, would be ineffective, inasmuch as the innocent is represented as being punished, while the guilty escape. It is objected that such an atonement prevents God forever from punishing a human being, inasmuch as having taken vengeance on one Being for human offences, He has no right to demand punishment a second time for the same offences. It is objected that Christ's sufferings, in view of His undoubted innocency, are an arbitrary and needless infliction, which reveals on the part of God a vindictive and sanguinary temper, inconsistent with the character of a Holy Being. It is objected that our own pre-supposition of the authority of God, as well as of His mercy, makes it necessary to believe that He has both the ability and the desire to forgive sins

Forgiveness without Sacrifice

without sacrifice; that we cannot imagine God to be less noble and generous than a man, who, having been injured, displays magnanimity, and freely, unconditionally forgives him who has done the injury, and who is incapable of repairing the injury he has done. It has been known that a man who, in a fit of passion, struck another and put out his eye, committing thus an injury he could not repair, was truly and unconditionally forgiven by his injured companion. Can we suppose, it is asked, that such magnanimity in a man is more godlike than God Himself? Are we not, then, driven to reject the Atonement, and to believe instead in forgiveness without sacrifice?

Of course these objections are, to a large extent, removed from the mind of a thoughtful and reasonable man the moment he is shown that they rest on an interpretation of the Bible teaching of the Divine Sacrifice, which need not be regarded as shutting out other interpretations. If the Bible can only be regarded as teaching that the Father is appeased by the death of the Son, then these foregoing objections appear to be unanswerable. But when it is seen that such interpretations are not necessary interpretations, but that one may hold, with the simple language of the Record, that the Father sent the Son, and commended His love to us in so doing, that the Son came in holy willingness as the supreme manifestation of the Father's purpose, and that, in the unity of the Godhead, the loving purpose of the Father to redeem and the loving act of the Son in redemption are but two inseparable sides of one idea; when this is shown to be an idea conformable with Scripture, then to a very large extent the foregoing objections are removed from a reasonable mind. There is no longer any occasion to

Forgiveness without Sacrifice

call in question the morality of God in exacting suffering from an innocent Being to satisfy anger stirred by the sins of the guilty. Such a conception of God vanishes like a grim nocturnal shadow before the dawn, and in the calm and holy light of truth one sees simply these three things: the holy love of God the Father for the beloved race of mankind; the holy wrath of God the Righteous against sin as an intolerable condition in the universe, calling, on moral grounds, for its condemnation in the punishment of those who commit it; the holy Sacrifice of Christ the God-man to meet on behalf of a beloved but sinful race that inevitable moral demand for the judgment and condemnation of sin.

In the calm, holy light of Bible truth, where stand revealed these three inseparable ideas: God the Loving, desiring the best for man; God the Righteous, condemning, by the moral necessity of His Being, sin

Forgiveness without Sacrifice

as an intolerable element in the universe; God the Sacrifice, enduring in Himself, by obedience unto death, that necessary condemnation of sin on behalf of a beloved race, — in the light of this truth we begin to read an answer to this great question: Why not forgiveness without sacrifice? The answer is this: Because of that moral necessity in the Nature of God which calls for the condemnation of sin. It cannot be necessary to defend with argument the proposition of such a moral necessity in the Nature of God as calls for the condemnation of sin. To some extent we are conscious of that moral necessity in ourselves, not only in moments of disgust and loathing following an evil indulgence, but also, and far more surely, in moments of spiritual strength and vision, when, lifted near to God, we have discerned, as from His side, the goodness of good and the sinfulness of sin. To some extent

Forgiveness without Sacrifice

we are conscious of that moral necessity as confessed in the life of the community and of the nation in its undying struggle after public righteousness, its eternal condemnation of public sin. But when we lift our thought to God the Righteous, the existence of a moral necessity in His Nature calling for the condemnation of sin becomes an axiom, a self-evident proposition transcending demonstration. Apart from it, God the Righteous is unthinkable. For there are but four attitudes possible in any being toward sin, — ignorance, indifference, consent, condemnation. God the Righteous cannot be ignorant; God the Righteous cannot be indifferent; God the Righteous cannot consent; God the Righteous must condemn, *must* under the moral necessity of His Being. But how is condemnation to be expressed? In two ways only is it expressible to man on the part of God,— through precept

Forgiveness without Sacrifice

and through penalty. When the first fails there remains only the second. God condemned sin by precept to the unfallen world: " Eat not of it, for in the day when thou eatest thereof, thou shalt surely die." The wrath of God was revealed from heaven against all sin, all ungodliness and unrighteousness of men. The judgment of God was known, that they which commit such things are worthy of death. The condemnation of sin through precept was universally published; it was written in the natural conscience, it was spoken in the law. God was true to the moral necessity of His Nature in openly condemning sin and warning against it. In vain; the freedom of man challenged the precept of God. " By one man sin entered into the world, and death by sin; and death passed upon all men, for that all have sinned." The condemnation of sin by penalty became, therefore, in the failure of precept, a moral neces-

Forgiveness without Sacrifice

sity in the nature of God the Righteous. He could not do otherwise. There is nothing of passion, nothing of revenge, nothing of hatred, nothing of sanguinary desire in God's punishing of sin. The punishment of sin is the condemnation of sin by penalty, its condemnation by precept having failed. Therefore to suggest forgiveness without sacrifice is to suggest a knowledge of sin on God's part unaccompanied by His condemnation of it. If it be true that there are but four attitudes toward sin, — ignorance, indifference, consent, or condemnation, — forgiveness without sacrifice would mean, apparently, sin without condemnation, leaving the alternatives of ignorance, of indifference, or of consent. Well has the Scripture said: "Without shedding of blood there is no remission."

But if all that has been thus far said has somewhat cleared the subject, there will remain in some minds

Forgiveness without Sacrifice

a serious question unanswered. Granting all that has been claimed in this chapter, how, in what sense, does the sacrifice of Christ atone for sin? Thus: the Holy Sacrifice of the God-Man meets, on behalf of a beloved but sinful race, that necessary moral demand in the Nature of God the Righteous for the judgment and condemnation of sin. "God, sending His own Son in the likeness of sinful flesh, and as an offering for sin, condemned sin in the flesh, that the requirement of the law (that is, the moral necessity which exists in God's Nature, that sin shall be condemned before it is forgiven) might be fulfilled in us, who walk not after the flesh, but after the Spirit." Here is the heart of the Gospel of the Divine Sacrifice. A moral necessity in the Nature of God requires sin's condemnation. The proclaiming of that condemnation in precept failed. It failed

Forgiveness without Sacrifice

through the inalienable freedom of man. There remained only penalty. Sin must be condemned unto death before it can be forgiven. The judgment of God is that they which commit such things are worthy of death. And the tender love of God has for us men, and for our salvation, met, through Christ, that moral necessity in the nature of God's righteousness which compels that sin be condemned unto death ere it can be forgiven. The Divine Sacrifice, the Death of Christ, is God's way of love to meet the moral demand of His own Being. The Death of Christ is God's condemnation of sin. Christ becoming obedient unto death, therein consents to that law of righteousness in God's Nature which condemns sin. That condemnation of sin was made on behalf of the whole race; He tasted death, He fulfilled the law of righteousness, for every man. And

Forgiveness without Sacrifice

<u>now</u> no obstacle remains in the path of God's forgiveness of sins but one, — the will of each individual man. Will the individual person identify himself with Christ in His Death by believing on Him as the Divine Sacrifice for sins? Will he begin to do this by the act of faith, that is, by voluntarily uniting himself to Christ in His obedience to the condemnation of sin, and by rising with Him into newness of life, henceforth to walk not after the flesh, but after the Spirit? Will he glorify the righteousness of God in the condemnation of sin by this identifying of himself with the Divine Sacrifice? Or will he turn away from the Christ hard in heart, proud in spirit, trusting in his own righteousness, venturing to believe that God will deny His Nature by forgiving sin without the solemn consent of the human will, in the act of faith, to the condemnation of sin by the Death

Forgiveness without Sacrifice

of Christ? Salvation appears to depend on this decision. Christ is our Shelter from the condemnation of sin. Disbelieving Him, we invite the penalty of sin upon ourselves. It is well to hear His own words, and to take them at their full value: " He that believeth on Him is not judged: He that believeth not hath been judged already, because he hath not believed on the Name of the Only Begotten Son of God."

IV

THE SORROW OF CHRIST IN HIS SACRIFICE

A Man of Sorrows.
>> PROPHECY OF ISAIAH.

Then cometh Jesus unto Gethsemane, and began to be sorrowful and sore troubled. Then saith He unto them, My soul is exceeding sorrowful, even unto death.
>> GOSPEL OF ST. MATTHEW.

Father, if Thou be willing, remove this cup from Me; nevertheless, not My Will, but Thine, be done.
>> GOSPEL OF ST. LUKE.

Ye shall drink indeed of My cup.
>> GOSPEL OF ST. MATTHEW.

That I may know Him, and the fellowship of His sufferings.
>> EPISTLE TO THE PHILIPPIANS.

Chapter IV

The Sorrow of Christ in His Sacrifice

It may be profitable, at this point, to review in outline the ground already traversed.

In entering upon a study of the Gospel of the Divine Sacrifice, we sought a starting-point from which to think our way up to Jesus Christ and Him crucified. We found what we sought in the proposition: The Atonement not the cause of God's Love, but Love the cause of the Atonement; not, God loves us because Christ died for us, but Christ died for us because God loves us. The Atonement was seen to be the supreme expression of God's eternal love for man; and the Unity of the Godhead was seen to be manifested

Sorrow of Christ in His Sacrifice

in the oneness of the Father's purpose in sending the Son to be the Saviour of the world, with the purpose of the Son in coming to redeem the world. From that starting-point we have made two considerable advances toward a reverential and humble interpretation of the Divine Sacrifice. We have investigated the Atonement as to the extent of its reference to mankind, and as to the necessity for its occurrence as a condition precedent to the forgiveness of sins. As to the extent of the Atonement in its reference to mankind, we conclude in the light of Scripture, that it is universal and not limited; that Christ died as the Redeemer of the whole world without distinction of persons, and not merely to secure the salvation of a selected portion of the human race. As to the necessity for the Atonement, as a condition precedent to the forgiveness of sins, we have asked a serious practical question —

Sorrow of Christ in His Sacrifice

Why not forgiveness without sacrifice? — and have thus answered it: Because of a moral necessity in the Nature of God the Righteous, calling for the condemnation of sin before they who have committed sin can be forgiven. We pointed out that there appear to be but four possible attitudes toward sin which can be taken by a rational being, — ignorance, indifference, consent, or condemnation. God the Righteous cannot be ignorant; He cannot be indifferent; He cannot consent; He must, therefore, by the moral necessity of His Being, pronounce upon sin the judgment of condemnation. We stated that the condemnation of sin on the part of God the Righteous is expressible to man in two ways, — by precept and by penalty; that the condemnation of sin by precept was God's first method, when, to an unfallen race, still standing before Him in the strength and beauty of primeval

Sorrow of Christ in His Sacrifice

innocence, He gave the clear warning that sin is an intolerable evil in His sight. We recalled the fact that the freedom of man challenged the precept of God by insisting upon the exercise of liberty in choices contrary to the will of God, thereby precipitating into human experience a condition of sin. God's condemnation of sin by precept having failed to deter man from making sin his own experience, and sin being forthwith a fact in human life, God's further condemnation of it by penalty was inevitable under the moral necessity in God's Nature by which He cannot consent to the existence of this intolerable evil. Death came by sin, as its penalty, its wages, a bodily and a spiritual doom, developed in the nature of the case through the antagonism of free beings to a Divine order of life. But that moral necessity in God which requires that sin shall be

Sorrow of Christ in His Sacrifice

condemned through penalty ere it can be forgiven, cannot be separated, even in our thought, from that eternal love in God which yearns to forgive the sinful. And the Atonement is the way whereby, in the Unity of the Godhead, eternal love satisfied the moral necessity of eternal righteousness. "God sending His own Son, in the likeness of sinful flesh, and as an offering for sin, condemned sin in the flesh;" *i.e.*, in the Incarnate Christ. The Sacrifice of the Incarnate Christ is an act of the Godhead, done in the Person of the Divine Son, on behalf of the human race, as a solemn condemnation of sin through death. On the Cross of Christ, in the Body and Soul of the Representative Man, the sin of man is judged and condemned unto death, as a thing intolerable in the universe of God; and thus eternal love itself meets the demand of eternal righteousness, and through a Divine Sacrifice, by enduring the condemnation of sin, makes possible its forgiveness. Every obstacle in the path of forgiveness is thus removed, save one, — the will of the individual. The race, as a race, is redeemed, in that the sins of the whole world are condemned in the Sacrifice of Christ, as the Representative of the race; but the individual, as an individual, the man, the woman, the child, is saved only when the personal will consents to the righteousness of sin's condemnation as accomplished in Christ's Sacrifice; when the person identifies himself or herself, by faith, with the humiliated, suffering, crucified Saviour; dying with Christ, as it were, unto sin, as unto an accursed and intolerable condition, and rising with Christ, as it were, unto newness of life, to walk not after the flesh, but after the Spirit. This recapitulation of the argument is found to have been

Sorrow of Christ in His Sacrifice

advantageous when we approach our present theme, which is the *Sorrow of Christ in His Sacrifice.* It is impossible to affirm the nature of His Sorrow without affirming the nature of His Sacrifice, and the nature of His Sacrifice depends on the constitution of His Person. What He suffered depends on what He did, and what He did depends on what He is.

Sorrow is one of the most elementary conditions of organic life in a world disordered by sin. Sin's disorder extends far beyond the confines of human life, as the rings on the lake spread in circles immensely greater than the stone dropped therein. Intelligence, human or prehuman, sins; creation suffers. "The whole creation groaneth and travaileth in pain." The Bible reveals sin as older and wider than humanity. The tragedy of Satan's fall is older than that of the race which

Sorrow of Christ in His Sacrifice

fell by a Satanic temptation. As the fossil secrets of the rocks are discovered, we find pain and sorrow were here, in the struggles and woes of the lower animals, ere there were human hearts to break or human eyes to weep.

Upon studying the great fact of sorrow, we find it to contain gradations and variations. Sorrows are differentiated not only in degree but in kind. Sorrows vary in kind where the beings who experience them vary in nature. The sorrow of a bird whose nest has been robbed, or of a beast whose young are slain before her eyes, are types of sorrow conditioned on the nature of the beast and the bird. The sorrow of a mother at the death-bed of her child includes, it may be, the instinctive grief of all living creatures in the destruction of their offspring,— but who will describe the sorrow of a bereaved human mother as differing only in degree from that of the animal whose young is slain? It is a difference in kind, conditioned on the superior nature of the human being, who, with a heart capable of nobler affection, a mind gifted with rational powers, a spirit competent to love or to hate God, transforms sorrow into something unknowable by an inferior order of being. As for the gradations of sorrow between beings possessing the same nature, such as, for example, human nature, it seems reasonable to look upon such gradations as differences in degree, rather than in kind. Frequently contrasts are drawn between the sorrows of the ignorant and unrefined and the sorrows of those whose natures have been highly trained, and the claim is made that culture removes, by a process of elevation, one part of the human race so far from the other parts of the human race, that the sorrows of cultivated natures differ in kind, as well as in degree, from those of the ignorant and uncultivated classes. This claim is a pleasing one from the point of view of educated humanity. It seems to reserve for refined natures a certain exclusiveness in grief as well as in pleasure. But as one grows to know humanity better, one questions the logic of this claim. It is true that conventional advantages and superior training tend to increase the capacity for experiencing certain forms of pleasure and of pain, as well as for manifesting certain types of joy and of sorrow; but he who in his study of humanity goes beneath these external differences, may expect to find the fundamental phenomena of sorrow the same in all who share the common nature.

Proceeding along this line of reasoning, we come at length to the Sorrow of Christ in His Sacrifice,

Sorrow of Christ in His Sacrifice

and to a thoughtful and inquiring mind, inclined to seek by investigation a basis for its faith rather than to accept without questioning the ancestral positions of historic belief, the very phrase, "the Sorrow of Christ" is a challenge to the reason. Why is it a challenge to the reason? Because it seems to make the Sorrow of Christ unique. Because, in a world filled with sorrow, where it is impossible to escape the incessant sights and sounds of grief, save by fleeing to the desert and leading a hermit's life; in a world where the tragic element is incessantly present, where forever some Rachel is weeping for her children, some human body is quivering in mortal anguish, some home is being plunged in new-made woe, some hopes are being grimly wrecked; in a world where some lives are always rising into awful prominence by reason of their extraordinary sorrow, the Sorrow of

Sorrow of Christ in His Sacrifice

Jesus Christ in His Sacrifice stands from age to age supreme and unapproached by any other grief of earth. The woes of more than five and twenty centuries have come and gone since he who was called the "Evangelical Prophet" composed that simple phrase, "a Man of Sorrows" as a portrait of Christ; and to-day, though millions of men have sorrowed since, there is in the thought of the world One, and only One, "Man of Sorrows." Millions of men have approached those great life-sorrows which stand like dark Gethsemanes in the path of human feet, yet to One, and to One only, do we feel the right, or even the inclination, to apply the words of that majestic narrative: "Then cometh He unto Gethsemane, and began to be sorrowful and sore troubled; Then saith He unto them, My soul is exceeding sorrowful, even unto death." This is a challenge to

Sorrow of Christ in His Sacrifice

the reason because it differentiates between the Sorrow of Christ and the sorrow of other beings in a manner which leaves little room for any other conclusion than that the Sorrow of Christ is believed to be different in kind from the sorrows of all other beings. It is not here forgotten that another conclusion has been reached by many gifted and refined minds touching the Sorrow of Christ. Full value should be given and due respect should be paid to the opinion of those, who, believing Christ to be the Son of God only in the sense of being the most Godlike of men, describe His Sacrifice as an heroic martyrdom for righteousness' sake, and His Sorrow as the grief of a beautiful soul, conquering its agony by patience and fortitude; and greater only in degree than the sorrows of others, because springing from a nature more pure and more heroic

Sorrow of Christ in His Sacrifice

than that of other men. One is impressed with the intellectual and moral beauty of many who have defended this Humanitarian View of the Person of Christ, but reason seems to be challenged by the facts of Christian history and by the declarations of Christian Scriptures to furnish some foundation broader and deeper than that of the sentiment of admiration to account for the supreme position which through eighteen centuries of theological changes has been steadily assigned to the Sorrow of Christ in His Sacrifice.

It was frankly stated at the outset of this study in Evangelical belief that the Authenticity of Scripture, the Inspiration of Scripture, and the Godhead of Christ are assumed. Proceeding on the basis of these assumptions (and they are here stated as assumptions only because time forbids a statement of the grounds on which they rest), it

Sorrow of Christ in His Sacrifice

must appear that the nature of Christ's Sorrow in His Sacrifice depends on the Nature of Christ's Person in His Incarnation. What He suffered depends on what He is. If His Nature is simply the most perfect example of our own nature, we are justified in looking upon His Sorrow as such as our own would be under similar circumstances, only greater in degree. If His Nature, beside including a perfect humanity, was also the Nature of the Godhead, then Christ's Sorrow in His Sacrifice, while on its human side such as man may to some extent experience, is also on its Divine side such as God only can experience; such as differs, not in degree alone, but in kind, from the sorrow of man.

Who, then, is this Man of Sorrows? He is God, clothed in human nature. Why has God clothed Himself in human nature? That He may stand visibly before men

Sorrow of Christ in His Sacrifice

as their Representative, and, as such, meet by death that moral necessity of God's righteousness which requires the condemnation of sin ere it can be forgiven. Christ is not a holy human being acting as God's Representative. Christ is God acting as man's Representative, by clothing Himself in man's nature, and suffering therein for man's sake. Christ is the Second Member of the Godhead, and the Unity of the Godhead is not interrupted by His Incarnation. He is continuously and forever, God the Son, One in Substance, One in Purpose, with God the Father. The attitude of the Godhead toward the human race is the attitude of love. In the Father that attitude finds expression when the Father sends the Son to be the Saviour of the world. In the Son, that attitude finds expression when the Son enters the world clothed in human nature, as man's

Sorrow of Christ in His Sacrifice

Representative, and saying by His very presence on earth: "Lo, I come to do the Father's will." The Person of Christ is, then, something utterly and absolutely unique. Never before was there, never afterwards could there be, another Christ. He stands alone, necessarily unique. "I am Alpha and Omega, the Beginning and the Ending, the First and the Last." In Him is our nature truly and veritably present; the power to think our thoughts, to know our experiences, to bear our griefs, to carry our sorrows. In Him is also the Nature of the Godhead truly and veritably present: the eternal love of the Godhead for the human race, purposing the glory of the race, sorrowing over its downfall; the eternal righteousness of the Godhead, moved, by the moral necessity of the Being of God, with everlasting wrath and antagonism against sin, as an intolerable condition in the universe. Assuming the Authenticity and Inspiration of the Holy Scripture, and speaking simply as a reporter of their contents, one must fearlessly say that the Scriptures require us to regard the Person of Christ as that of God clothed in human nature, real humanity coexisting with veritable and unqualified Godhead. His assumption of humanity is not accomplished by His resignation of Godhead. He does not become man by ceasing to be God, but in the uninterrupted life and consciousness of His Godhead He assumes once and forever the nature of man; for three and thirty years, carrying it amidst conditions of humiliation consummated in death, and thence. onward and eternally, carrying it in the power and blessedness of Risen Glory. Upon the basis of such a doctrine of the Person of Christ

Sorrow of Christ in His Sacrifice

it is easy to foresee the conclusions which must follow concerning the Sorrow of Christ in His Sacrifice. What He suffered depends on what He is. Granting that the Person of Christ is the Person of the God-Man, the conclusions are irresistible touching the nature of His sorrow. The Sorrow of Christ in His Sacrifice is the sorrow of man under conditions of supreme humiliation. The Sorrow of Christ in His Sacrifice is the Sorrow of God making Atonement for sin. Into these conclusions we must look.

The Sorrow of Christ in His Sacrafice is the sorrow of man under conditions of supreme humiliation. Human hearts in all ages have been drawn to the Cross by the power of sympathy. The appeal of that marvellous countenance of the Man of Sorrows, marred by the ravages of grief, has always been, to multitudes, irresistible. Has it been an illusion

Sorrow of Christ in His Sacrifice

or a mistake that we have seemed to see in the Man of Sorrows something we could understand, something that could understand us? Has it been an error that even many of us Protestants cannot stand unmoved before the crucifix, nor doubt that in some manner that emblem of the grief of the Sacrifice takes hold upon our hearts? Is it a dream, which a better knowledge of Him might dissolve, that when we have suffered in our temptations, tossed in our feverish sickness, trembled in the loneliness of our responsibilities, wept in secret over our public humiliations, or sat speechless and stonelike to watch the ashen pallor of death change the face of our dearly loved one, we have been calmed, if not composed, by the thought of the Sorrow of Christ? Was there nothing real in the instinct which bade us bring Him into places in our life, too deep, too dark, too dreary for

Sorrow of Christ in His Sacrifice

others to enter; which prompted us to believe that His experience of sorrow had preceded and could comprehend our own? It was not a dream.) It was not an error. The Sorrow of Christ was the sorrow of man, and as such, it is supreme among the sorrows of men and precious to all men of sorrows. Supreme and precious because the perfection of His Humanity enabled Him without let or hindrance to explore, through experience, the possibilities of sorrow. We have only to remember the sensitiveness, the purity, the affectionateness, the aspiration of the Manhood of Jesus to perceive the acuteness and the manifoldness of the Sorrow of His whole life. And in the unspeakable sadness of His Sacrifice the sorrows extended over a lifetime seem to be compressed and intensified; — the sorrow of temptation which, because of His undefiled Soul, was more awful to Him than it could

Sorrow of Christ in His Sacrifice

be to a sinner; the sorrow of intellectual and spiritual loneliness as His Soul swelled with thoughts and feelings not to be uttered because even the best and brightest of His friends could not bear them then; the sorrow of realizing about Him an atmosphere of hatred and distrust, when His own heart was charged with love and faithfulness; the sorrow of being despised and rejected of men, loaded with ignominy, repulsed with bitterness; the sorrow of an enforced contact with sin, the thing that He hated and loathed, yet the thing that was pressed on His attention at every turn; the sorrow of confronting in all the beauty of His young Manhood a death most horribly devised by the very genius of cruelty; the sorrow of beholding His friends betray Him, deny Him, and desert Him, leaving Him to face that bloody death, scorned by the Jew, scourged by the Gentile. Yes!

Sorrow of Christ in His Sacrifice

The Sorrow of Christ in His Sacrifice was the sorrow of man; it was the sorrow, greater in degree than ours, yet the same in kind, the sorrow of our Brother, of our Friend, Who, because in His sensitive, holy Humanity He has explored the possibilities of earthly sorrow, can come so marvellously into the sacred places of our human thought and be to us what none else can be.

But was it only the sorrow of man? Was it not this and also more than this? Yes! The Sorrow of Christ in His Sacrifice was the Sorrow of God making Atonement for sin. The Sorrow of God? Is such a thing possible as the Sorrow of God? Can God be in sorrow? To those whose conception of God has been such as to swallow up the idea of the Fatherhood in that of the Sovereignty, to those who have unconsciously lost their sense of the Unity of the Godhead by contrasting

Sorrow of Christ in His Sacrifice

God with Christ, God as hating man and wishing to destroy him, Christ as loving man and dying to save him, it is difficult to realize the Sorrow of God. And we do not realize it until we firmly grasp that fundamental idea, the Unity of the Godhead; that the love, the tenderness, and the sorrow we find in God the Son, must also be in God the Father, and that because Christ is of the Nature of the Godhead, the Sorrow of Christ is the Sorrow of God, making Atonement for sin. But are there any words competent to set forth in any degree a thought so vast as the thought of the Sorrow of God in the Atonement? There would not be were it not for the fulness with which the Scriptures reveal the purpose of God toward man and the attitude of God toward sin. But through the revelation of those Scriptures we can, even to some small extent, conceive of the Sorrow of God.

Sorrow of Christ in His Sacrifice

We behold in it the Sorrow of distress for the Fall of man; the Sorrow of wrath for the wilfulness of man; the Sorrow of humiliation in bearing the curse of sin.

The Sorrow of God in the Divine Sacrifice was the Sorrow of distress for the Fall of man. When, in one of our human homes, a beloved child goes wrong, and, choosing darkness rather than light, breaks away from parental love, what distress comes to a father's, to a mother's heart! And if we can suffer so in the failure of our dear ones, what must God suffer in the falling of the race? The measure of that grief must be the love that inspired God's glorious purpose for man. When man set himself against that purpose he pierced the heart of God. And that Sorrow of God in the falling of the race was the sorrow of an infinite knowledge which could foresee the interminable evolution of sin's results in the human

Sorrow of Christ in His Sacrifice

race, the foul and loathsome perversion of the laws of our being, the devilish riot of unchastened desires, the doom of heredity, blighting unborn generations. Because in Christ dwelt the fulness of the Godhead bodily, we know that He saw all this, felt all this, knew all this, as He lived among the fallen race, and then went forth to die at the hands of the fallen race, bearing upon His Divine Self-consciousness a full knowledge of the misery sin had caused and yet would cause.

The Sorrow of God in the Divine Sacrifice was the Sorrow of wrath for the wilfulness of man. The Fall was the calamity of the beloved race; but the Fall was also the sin of the beloved race, the wilfulness of wills made in the image of God's will and erecting themselves in revolt and defiance against the will of God. By a moral necessity of the Godhead, wrath and condemnation are

Sorrow of Christ in His Sacrifice

poured upon sin, as an intolerable evil in the universe. They which commit such things are worthy of death. The wrath of God is revealed from heaven upon all ungodliness of men. And because in Christ dwelt the fulness of the Godhead bodily, His attitude and feeling towards sin and sinfulness as He went to His Cross were the attitude and feeling of Godhead. He recognized, as the cause of His death, sin, the one thing that God hates, and against which His wrath is poured out; and as He beheld Himself surrounded by a race glorying in sin, pushing their sin upon His notice, flaunting their wilfulness in His face, to what marvellous proportions rises the tragedy of the Atonement, when we see the wrath of the Godhead and the meekness of the Lamb blending in Christ's Soul.

The Sorrow of God in the Divine

Sorrow of Christ in His Sacrifice

Sacrifice was the Sorrow of humiliation in bearing the curse of sin. He humbled Himself and became obedient unto death, even the death of the Cross. Oh! the awfulness of that humiliation! God the Righteous bowing down under sin, the thing which He hated, and receiving upon Himself, as if He were a sinner, the curse and condemnation of sin. No wonder that even God Himself faltered before that intolerable humiliation. No wonder that Christ, in Whom the Godhead dwelt, when He realized that the hour had come when that humiliation under sin must be publicly disclosed in the horrors of Calvary, that He must drink that deadly cup of wrath in the sight of men, sank in the darkness of the Garden, a sweat of blood breaking from Him, and prayed: "O my Father, if it be possible, let this cup pass from Me!" No wonder, when

Sorrow of Christ in His Sacrifice

the shame of that humiliation was actively experienced in the nakedness of the Cross, it seemed to Him that Godhead Itself was blotted out as with a cloud, and he cried: "My God, my God, why hast Thou forsaken Me!"

What shall our relation be to the Sorrow of Christ in His Sacrifice? Can there be one who, having followed this thought, remains in entire indifference? Can there be one content to regard this theme in a spirit of impassive speculation,—content to gaze at the Sorrow of that Sacrifice with no responsive emotion, with naught but intellectual curiosity? Can there be one content to give to the Sorrowing Saviour only sentimental pity, one who is not lifted by the conception of the Sorrow of God to a plane of thought where pity dies in awe?

Well may one pray for power

Sorrow of Christ in His Sacrifice

to understand what Christ meant when He said: "Ye shall drink of my cup;" what an Apostle sought when he cried, "That I may know Him and the fellowship of His sufferings." How can man have a fellowship with sufferings that are the Sufferings of God? Only by self-abasement in the presence of those Sufferings, being crucified with Christ by the sacrifice of the will, condemning sin in oneself, and by faith uniting oneself to Him in His Death, that one may be raised with Him in His Resurrection, to walk with Him in newness of life.

V

THE JOY OF CHRIST IN HIS SACRIFICE

Who, for the joy that was set before Him, endured the cross, despising the shame.
>> EPISTLE TO THE HEBREWS.

And I, if I be lifted up from the earth, will draw all men unto Me. This He said, signifying what death He should die."
>> GOSPEL OF ST. JOHN.

Be of good cheer; I have overcome the world.
>> GOSPEL OF ST. JOHN.

When He cometh into the world He saith, sacrifice and offering Thou wouldest not, but a Body didst Thou prepare for me. Then said I, Lo, I am come (in the roll of the book it is written of me) to do Thy Will, O God.
>> EPISTLE TO THE HEBREWS.

Chapter V

The Joy of Christ in His Sacrifice

WE now approach a theme which, in the nature of the case, stands in close relation to that of the preceding chapter. Whatever observations we may be permitted to make touching the Joy of Christ in His Sacrifice, must necessarily rest upon the same belief concerning the Nature of His Person as that which supported us in our study of the Sorrow of Christ in His Sacrifice. For the Sorrow of Christ and the Joy of Christ are two phases of personality revealed in one and the same Person. He Who knew the sorrow is He Who knew the joy. And as the elements of His Sorrow were conditioned on the qualities of

The Joy of Christ in His Sacrifice

His Person, as what He suffered depends on what He is; so the elements of His Joy are conditioned equally on the qualities of His Person, and the nature of His Joy depends on what He is. We have already affirmed our belief concerning the constitution of the Person of Jesus Christ, the Mediator. We have asked and have answered the question, "Who, then, is the Man of Sorrows?" We have replied: "He is God, clothed in human nature." We have said (and there is an obvious propriety in refreshing our memories as to the exact position taken): "The Person of Christ is absolutely and necessarily unique. Never before was there, never afterward could there be, another Christ. He is Alpha and Omega, the Beginning and the Ending, the First and the Last. In Him is our nature truly and veritably present, — the power to think our thoughts, to

The Joy of Christ in His Sacrifice

know our experiences, to bear our griefs, to carry our sorrows. In Him is also the Nature of Godhead truly and veritably present, the eternal love of the Godhead for the human race, purposing the glory of the human race, sorrowing over its downfall; the eternal righteousness of the Godhead, moved, by the moral necessity of the Being of God, with everlasting wrath and antagonism against sin, as an intolerable condition in the universe. The Person of Christ (such appears to be the actual teaching of the Scripture) is real Humanity co-existing with veritable and unqualified Godhead; His assumption of the humanity is not accomplished by His resignation of the Godhead. He does not become man by ceasing temporarily to be God; but in the uninterrupted life of His Godhead, He assumed once and forever the nature of man, carrying it for three and thirty years

The Joy of Christ in His Sacrifice

amidst conditions of humiliation consummated in death, and thence, onward and eternally, carrying it in the power and blessedness of Risen Glory." (See Chapter IV.)

One can well understand how it may be difficult for some to join in this affirmation of belief who nevertheless reverence and adore the Person of Christ as Divine. The difficulty encountered by these minds is that of conceiving how Christ could be truly man while at the same moment truly self-conscious of His Eternal Godhead. It seems necessary to those feeling this difficulty to regard Him as having laid aside His Godhead when, to quote the noble language of the Philippian Epistle, " He, being in the form of God, counted it not a prize to be on an equality with God, but emptied Himself, taking the form of a servant, being made in the likeness of men." " What," it is asked, " can that mean,

The Joy of Christ in His Sacrifice

if not that He emptied Himself of His Godhead and became, for the time being, merely a man?" "How," it is asked, "can we hold the blessed truth of a Christ made like unto His earthly brethren, unless we also hold that whilst He tarried on the earth His humiliation was in the fact that He had laid off His Godhead?"

It can hardly be necessary to point out that this view of the Person of Christ is far removed from that humanitarian view of His Person which feels that it has made its utmost concession when it grants Him to have been only the loveliest and the most godlike of the children of men. This humanitarian view is the exaltation of a man among his fellow-men by his supremacy in human virtues; the other view is the humiliation of a God down to the rank of men, by His voluntary abdication of Godhead. The two opinions are as far from one another

The Joy of Christ in His Sacrifice

as is the east from the west. But, as one examines without preconceptions or prejudices the scriptures which describe the Person of Christ, one sees reasons, lifting themselves out of the very Word, and expanding above one like the outstretched wings of God, why the humiliation of Jesus Christ could not have consisted in the laying off of His conscious Godhead; why, on the contrary, it must have consisted in retaining the self-conscious Godhead and affiliating it, in infinite self-abasement, with the nature of men. If Jesus Christ is, in fact, a Member of the Godhead, can He at any time cease, for a season, from that existence? Can the Godhead be, in any sense, or in any part of its Selfhood, intermittent? If Jesus Christ is the Mediator between God and man, could He be that without uniting in Himself the two natures between which He is to mediate?

The Joy of Christ in His Sacrifice

Could He reconcile man to God, could He reveal God to man, by ceasing to be God? But still greater and more conclusive reasons present themselves. If Christ's humiliation consisted in laying off His Godhead, in His emptying Himself of Godhead, then it follows that through the whole process of His mediatorial work on earth, and in the very consummation of that work, in His Sacrifice, He was deprived of all mediatorial and Divine self-consciousness of the significance and value of His own acts. He knew not what He did, save as a man might know the impulse of self-sacrifice. As He hung in that wild storm, when the waves of human hatred and rejection broke against His Cross, did His dormant Godhead slumber on, unconscious that a world was in the very act and article of its Redemption? And, greater than all other thoughts, if

The Joy of Christ in His Sacrifice

Christ's humiliation was the laying off of Godhead, if His sorrow in death is but the dying sorrow of a human self-consciousness, then what is there in His Sacrifice to constitute it an Atonement for the world? Wherein, then, does His death differ from the death of other heroes? Nay! the humiliation of Christ is not the laying off of Godhead, but the retaining of Godhead in humiliating association with an inferior nature. The Sorrow of Christ is not in the temporary suspension of His Divine Self-consciousness, but in the preservation of that Divine Self-consciousness in the presence of repugnant and revolting experiences. The sorrow of human suffering on the surgeon's table is suspended when self-consciousness is put to sleep by the anæsthetic, but the Sorrow of the Divine Sacrifice is not suspended in the Person of the Son of God by the anæsthetic of renun-

The Joy of Christ in His Sacrifice

ciation in respect of His self-conscious Godhead. His humiliation and His Sorrow are in this: all that He is He knows Himself to be. And through the humiliation of this unalleviated self-knowledge in the Person of Christ, consciously active in the presence of sin, is the Atonement; for the Atonement is an Atonement because it is such an actual and suffering condemnation of sin on the part of God Himself as shall satisfy that moral necessity in the Nature of God which demands sin's condemnation ere sin's forgiveness is possible.

While we have thus been dwelling on the Sorrow of Christ in His Sacrifice, we have come, not merely to the threshold, but into the glorious heart of our present theme, — the Joy of Christ in His Sacrifice. For whatsoever in the constitution of His Person caused His Sorrow to be all that it was, is the same as

The Joy of Christ in His Sacrifice

that which caused His Joy to be all that it was, when He set His face steadfastly to go to Jerusalem, royal and exultant in spirit, as a King going to His coronation. We have seen that the Sorrow of Christ in His Sacrifice was the sorrow of man under conditions of supreme humiliation; and that it was also the sorrow of God making Atonement for sin. So may we also affirm: the Joy of Christ in His Sacrifice was the joy of man under conditions of heroic unselfishness; it was also the Joy of God in the Redemption and the Recovery of a beloved race.

Perhaps the most suggestive utterance in the New Testament concerning the Joy of the Mediator in His Sacrifice is that which in the Epistle to the Hebrews exhorts us to look unto Jesus as "the perfect example of that faith which we are to imitate."[1] Christ is there de-

---
[1] Wescott, Ep. to the Hebrews, p. 395.

The Joy of Christ in His Sacrifice

scribed as the One "Who, for the Joy that was set before Him, endured the Cross, despising the shame." The suggestions awakened in the mind when it perceives the force of that glorious expression, "the Joy that was set before Him," are exalting and gladdening. Jesus is there represented as enduring the Cross with noblest dignity, disregarding the judgment of men concerning the shame of the Cross, because, raised in spirit above the common levels of human perception, He beheld, set before Him, stretched out like a sunny landscape before His eyes, a vision of results proceeding from His Passion, which filled Him with joy. And so vast and substantial were these results as He realized them prospectively from His Cross, He was enabled, in the joy of them, to endure His sufferings, and to triumph even in His humiliation. Who can think of the Joy of Christ

The Joy of Christ in His Sacrifice

in His Sacrifice without desiring to know the sources and the nature of that Joy? Where such a desire exists, it may to some extent be satisfied. Our knowledge of human nature on its nobler side permits us to understand in some degree the Joy of Christ which His Humanity knew, and the Scriptures splendidly disclose the Joy that entered His Self-consciousness of Godhead even amidst the humiliation and sorrow of the Divine Sacrifice.

We have said that the Joy of Christ in His Sacrifice was the joy of man under conditions of heroic unselfishness. When we spoke of His Sorrow as a Man, a sorrow the more exquisitely keen because experienced in the purest and finest of natures, a sorrow including temptation; intellectual and spiritual loneliness; the hatred, distrust, and rejection of men; enforced contact with sin; the approach of a hor-

The Joy of Christ in His Sacrifice

rible death, accentuated by betrayal, denial, and desertion at the hands of His friends, — we perceived how these things, by being a part of Our Lord's experience, have accounted for that instinct in ourselves which bids us bring Him into places in our life too deep, too dark, too dreary for others to enter; which prompts us to believe that His experience of sorrow has comprehended our own. The Joy which was set before Him in His Sacrifice was in part this: that He perceived with the delight of heroic unselfishness how His sufferings were preparing Him an access into human hearts, an avenue to their deepest confidence. To one who deeply loves humanity, whose passion is the passion of helpfulness, there are moments when our suffering, whether of mind or body, seems worth all it costs, because of the added power that comes through it to understand

The Joy of Christ in His Sacrifice

those who suffer, and to gain their confidence. Though we may have known hours of darkness, hours of humiliation, hours when the burden of living seemed greater than we could bear, who regrets the sufferings of those hours, if, by means of them, one learned to read the secret of humanity's sorrow in a way that fitted one to meet humanity's need? This was the Joy of Christ as a Man, because He was a lover of men. In every temptation that stung like an arrow in the living flesh, in every bitter hour of loneliness, in every enforced contact with sin's revolting conditions, in every shock to friendship and affront to love, as friend after friend denied Him or turned the back and fled, in the darkling hour of impending death, in the last ecstatic agony of pain, He, the Lover of men, saw but one bond more, binding Him closer to humanity; but

The Joy of Christ in His Sacrifice

one pang more, helping Him to understand the hardship of life; but one claim more upon the affection and confidence of His brother-men; and so, for the joy that was set before Him, spreading far and long like a tender and sun-bathed landscape, the joy of winning men through sympathy with their condition, He endured the Cross, despising the shame.

But when we remember that in the Person of Christ dwelt not only the heroic unselfishness of a large and loving soul, but also the august Self-consciousness of Godhead, it is manifest that the Joy of Jesus in His Sacrifice is something infinitely broader and deeper than we have yet considered; for it is the Joy of God in the Redemption and the Recovery of a beloved race. To attempt the faintest delineation of that Mediatorial Joy, that Gladness of God, apart from the Scriptures,

The Joy of Christ in His Sacrifice

were indeed perilous, not to say presumptuous; for who hath known the mind of the Lord? But when our thought is founded on and limited by the Scriptures we may, without presumption, rise even to the plane of this magnificent conception, — the Joy of Jesus, as, self-conscious of His own Godhead, He beheld the purpose of His Incarnation attained through Sacrifice. Broader even than the measure of man's mind is the breadth of this thought. Yet, while we cannot comprehend it all, we may comprehend some of it. We may look, as if with His eyes, upon some part of that great landscape of Joy which He saw from the eminence of the Cross. He rejoiced in the doing of the Will of the Father. He rejoiced in the reconstruction of human society. He rejoiced in the communication of the spirit of victory to individual lives.

The Joy of Christ in His Sacrifice

He rejoiced in the doing of the Will of the Father. If we comprehend the meaning of that statement, we advance immensely toward a right understanding of the Gospel of the Divine Sacrifice. And to comprehend it is well within our power if we use the Scriptures. Men have talked wildly of the Will of God. But let us learn what Jesus tells us of the Will of God; Jesus, Who taught us to pray, saying: " Our Father Which art in heaven, Thy Will be done on earth as it is in heaven." Jesus came to do, to further, to accomplish the Will of God. So says the Scripture: " When He cometh into the world He saith: Sacrifice and offering Thou wouldest not, but a Body didst Thou prepare for Me. Then said I, Lo! I am come (in the roll of the Book it is written of Me) to do Thy Will, O God." The Will of the Father was in

The Joy of Christ in His Sacrifice

harmony with the Will of the Son. "I and My Father are One," says Christ; "I do always such things as please Him." There is no conflict, no distinction of motives, between the Father and Christ. The will of the Father is precious and acceptable to the Son. "My meat," says Christ, is to do the Will of Him that sent Me, and to finish His Work." Christ is not, in His Love, preventing, by sacrifice, a malignant Father from carrying out His wrathful Will. Christ, in His Love, is assisting and enabling, by sacrifice, a loving Father to carry out His blessed Will. What then is the Will of God of which the Son says: "Lo, I come to do Thy Will"? Westcott grandly expressed it, when he said: "The Will of God answers to the fulfilment of man's true destiny; and this, as things actually are, in spite of the Fall. Christ, as Son of Man, made this

The Joy of Christ in His Sacrifice

Will His own, and accomplished it."[1] The Will of God is the Eternal Purpose and choice on behalf of a beloved race that it shall be holy and therefore happy. Sin comes as a catastrophe, a self-ruin, upon the race. But sin, while it calls forth God's wrath, has no power to change God's Will. Yet sin stands in the way of that Will, forbidding its fulfilment. But because God is greater than sin, He will not have His Purpose blocked by sin. His Will shall be done; the race having fallen shall be redeemed and recovered to an estate where the Will of God can be done. We have studied the method of Redemption. We have seen that it is accomplished by an act of the Godhead, prompted wholly by love, wherein sin is condemned in the sacrifice of One, in Whom dwelleth all the fulness of the Godhead

[1] Wescott, Ep. to the Hebrews, p. 311.

The Joy of Christ in His Sacrifice

bodily. The Atonement is, then, one stage in the doing of the Will of God, the sweeping away of one vast obstacle reared in the path of that Will by the lawlessness of Satan and of man. When sin has been condemned in the Divine Sacrifice, that stage in the doing of the Will is finished, and Christ cries from the Cross, "It is finished," and the Joy of Christ in His Sacrifice is the Joy of God in the advancement, to a new stage of fulfilment, in spite of the Fall, of the Eternal Will of the Godhead for the beloved race. When Christ faltered in the garden, before the unsupportable humiliation of the Godhead, in being brought low beneath the condemnation of sin, when, in that hideous contact with evil, He cried: "If it be possible let this cup pass from Me!" then He remembered that only thus, only through this profoundest of all humiliations could

The Joy of Christ in His Sacrifice

the Will be done, could the condemnation of sin be effected without the doom of the race; and loving God's Will for the race above all else, He says: " Thy Will be done!" Then, when He came to the Cross, He saw before Him the spectacle of that redeemed and recovered race, placed by His own obedience to death in a position where sin can be forgiven, where God's Will can be done, and rejoicing in that thought He endured the Cross, despising the shame.

Christ rejoiced in the reconstruction of human society. " I, if I be lifted up from the earth, will draw all men unto Me." " This He said," adds St. John, "signifying what death He should die." It seems impossible to doubt that the Person of Christ contained the Self-consciousness of Godhead when we stand in the presence of such words as these: " I, if I be lifted up, will

The Joy of Christ in His Sacrifice

draw all men unto Me." If He were indeed emptied of Godhead by His Incarnation, so that He spake and reasoned but with the foresight of a man, then the significance of these words, as conceived in His own mind, approaches madness. Thus to speak of the result of His own death seems to involve an almost irrational confidence in the charm of His personal influence, an almost irrational contempt of those great time forces which, with the icy calm of the relentless glacier, slowly and surely override and bury all human influence that has not incorporated itself either in the literary life or in the political life of the world. Christ had not deified Himself by literary mastership; He had not imperialized Himself by a political *coup d'état*; He had nothing wherewith to hold the world but His pure and simple Personality. Could He rationally hope still to hold the

The Joy of Christ in His Sacrifice

world when the grave had closed over that Personality? Yet He says: " I, if I be lifted up from the earth, will draw all men unto Me." He spoke with the self-consciousness of Godhead, and so speaking He beheld, with a joy that made even the Cross and its shame despicable, how His Divine Sacrifice should become a new centre around which a race, disorganized by sin in all its thought and motives, might rally itself again, and reconstruct a new social order on a basis of purity, truth, self-sacrifice, and love. He saw from His Cross all that we, in our day, are seeing; how, wherever Christ is lifted up in all the fulness of His Divine Sacrifice, men and women are given a new desire to break from sin, a new longing to be like God, a new tenderness and care for one another. He saw what we have not yet seen, because the time of it has not yet come, — the future

The Joy of Christ in His Sacrifice

magnificence, catholicity, and peace of a Messianic Kingdom, where all shall know Him from the least to the greatest, where all shall be one in Him, in the unity of consecration and obedience, even as He is One with the Father, in the unity of the Eternal Godhead.

Christ rejoiced in the communication of the Spirit of Victory to individual lives. "Be of good cheer, I have overcome the world." Oh! most wondrous of all thoughts, to think that He saw, from His Cross, all that that Cross should come to mean to all who know its power, as a sign of Victory! He saw the weary and heavy-laden, toiling with leaden feet along the path of life, discouraged, overwelmed, doubting if life be worth the living, chilled by human neglect, stung by human unkindness, ready to sink; yet in that very hour catching sight of the Cross, feeling the thrill of its

The Joy of Christ in His Sacrifice

message through their souls, rising with new light in the eye, new strength in the will, new peace in the soul, because the Crucified had said: "Be of good cheer, I have overcome the world." He saw the man, the woman, the child, pressed by Satan to the verge of self-abandonment, caught in the toils and meshes of unmentionable temptation, feverish with conflicting passions, scorning self for the desire to yield, yet ready to yield because self had been scorned and trifled with too often; then, on the very verge of failure, remembering the Cross and beating down Satan under the feet, because the Crucified had said: "Be of good cheer, I have overcome the world." He saw the eyes that wept till there were no more tears to shed, the broken hearts that envied the dead resting in grassy graves, "Far from the madding crowd," the empty hands and emptier lives that had

The Joy of Christ in His Sacrifice

buried all that kept them busy, all that made them want to live; the shattered nerves that had no volition to take up life again : yet when grief refused to be comforted, when misery refused to think of aught except itself, the tearless eyes saw that Cross, and the broken heart resolved to be unselfish in its sorrow and to live for others, because the Crucified had said : " Be of good cheer, I have overcome the world." He saw the pallid faces of the dying, the thin hands that clung so wistfully to life, the eyes that closed in terror at each thought of the advancing shadow; the minds distracted with natural dread, conceiving of death but as the deafening whirlpool that engulfs a struggling wretch; yet when all was darkest and most confused, the Cross was held before those closing eyes, light came on those pallid faces, peace folded those clinging hands, rest composed those

The Joy of Christ in His Sacrifice

frightened minds, because the Crucified had said: " Be of good cheer, I have overcome the world!"

Oh! Joyful Christ! Oh! Happy Man of Sorrows! Well might Thine Heart exult even as it broke upon the Cross! For what glory lay before Thee in Thy death; — the doing of God's dear Will, the rebuilding of a social order, the communication of victory to innumerable souls, — well became it Thee to rejoice; — much was before Thee! "When Thou hadst overcome the sharpness of death Thou didst open the Kingdom of Heaven to all believers. When Thou ascendedst up on High, Thou didst lead captivity captive — Thou gavest gifts unto men!"

VI

THE REJECTION OF THE ATONEMENT

If any man hear My sayings, and keep them not, I judge him not; for I came not to judge the world, but to save the world. He that rejecteth Me, and receiveth not My sayings, hath one that judgeth him; the word that I spake, the same shall judge him in the last day. For I spake not from Myself, but the Father which sent Me, He hath given Me a commandment, what I should say and what I should speak.
GOSPEL OF ST. JOHN.

All men should honor the Son, even as they honor the Father. He that honoreth not the Son, honoreth not the Father which hath sent Him.
GOSPEL OF ST. JOHN.

He that rejecteth Me, rejecteth Him that sent Me.   GOSPEL OF ST. LUKE.

He that believeth on the Son of God hath the witness in Him; He that believeth not God, hath made Him a liar; because he hath not believed in the witness that God hath borne concerning His Son. And the witness is this, that God gave unto us Eternal Life, and this life is in His Son.   FIRST EPISTLE OF ST. JOHN.

A man that hath set at naught Moses' Law dieth without compassion on the word of two or three witnesses: of how much sorer punishment, think ye, shall he be judged worthy who hath trodden under foot the Son of God, and hath counted the Blood of the Covenant wherewith he was sanctified an unholy thing, and hath done despite unto the Spirit of Grace?
EPISTLE TO THE HEBREWS.

Chapter VI

The Rejection of the Atonement

ONE who studies the Gospel of the Divine Sacrifice must deal with the problem of the Rejection of the Atonement by the human understanding. The question is raised in the New Testament itself, in the First Epistle of Peter: " What shall be the end of them that obey not the Gospel of God? " For a logical mind, there is no escape from that question, be the attitude what it may toward the Gospel. Every mind that hears the Gospel must dispose in some way of that which it has heard, because the Gospel is an appeal to every mind. The person addressed may, on the one hand, accept, or may, on the other hand,

The Rejection of the Atonement

reject, the propositions submitted to him in the Gospel of the Divine Sacrifice. In either case he is entitled to his opinion. But every mind, whether in the attitude of acceptance or of rejection, must face the problem of rejection, and must reach a conclusion concerning the consequences of rejection. The conclusion reached by one may be that there are no consequences of importance attached to the rejection of the Atonement; that the Atonement may be regarded as incredible, and as such may be dismissed from the mind even as a thousand other matters are set aside, without involving the life in any present or future trouble. The conclusion reached by another may be that the Atonement is a message from God to man, involving personal redemption, and that he who sets the Atonement aside must ultimately reckon with God in the position of one who has

The Rejection of the Atonement

rejected God's message and refused God's mercy. These are opposite conclusions; and as a matter of personal liberty, each mind is entitled to hold whichever conclusion it chooses to hold.

Between two individuals holding opposite views on this subject, there is no ground for quarrel or dispute. But neither is there ground for complaint if one shall state frankly to the other what he believes to be involved in the rejection of the Atonement.

For example: It is within the power of a free being now and henceforth to reject the Atonement, but he not only may not wish to do it, because he has found Christ precious; he may not dare to do it, because he stands in terror of the consequences involved in so doing. No just charge of hardness or severity can be laid against such a free being, if he says what he believes for

The Rejection of the Atonement

himself concerning the peril of rejecting the Atonement. Every word he may say concerning the outlook for those who reject the Atonement becomes instantly applicable to himself, if he eventually takes the position of rejection. He is only saying frankly to others what he would wish another frankly to say to him, for the warning and the salvation of his soul. We will approach the subject in perfect candor, and if we feel constrained to carry the subject to its conclusions, we will give our reasons for entertaining such conclusions.

Before taking up, on their merits, the grounds and the consequences of rejecting the Atonement, a sense of the seriousness of the theme requires a definition of the word "rejection," and also calls for a statement of the authority upon which one ventures to speak to one's fellow-men of what is involved

The Rejection of the Atonement

in this rejection. Every student of English knows that the word "reject" means to "throw away," or "to cast from one," or "to discard" or "to refuse to acknowledge." Through all these shades of meaning, graded from a violent repudiation to a more or less calm and steady opposition, runs one common idea, — the will antagonizing a proposition presented to it. Rejection, be it violent or be it calm, implies the presentation of a subject to the mind, the consideration of that subject in the mind, and the opposition of that subject by the will. A mind incapable, for any reason, of considering a subject, cannot be described as having rejected it by not having given an assent, which it is, in fact, incapable of giving. Nor can a mind in ignorance of a proposition be said to have rejected that proposition by not having assented to that of

The Rejection of the Atonement

which it as yet knows nothing. The idea of rejecting the Atonement is, obviously, limited in important ways by these considerations. Multitudes who have died, or who still live in the earth, without giving their assent to the Atonement, have never rejected it. In many cases they were mentally incapable of considering it. In many other cases they remained in ignorance of it. The countless little children living in infancy upon the earth, or gathered, as we assuredly believe, in our Saviour's Presence, did not reject that which their undeveloped minds had no power to consider. The multitudes suffering from mental disease could not reject that which they were incapable of apprehending. And so, also, of ignorance. The generations of heathen races before which the Cross was never presented were not rejecters of Christ. "How," says St. Paul,

The Rejection of the Atonement

"shall they believe on Him of Whom they have not heard?" and we might add, How shall they reject an Atonement which they have not an opportunity to consider? And the same must be said of ignorance in Christian lands that is said of ignorance in heathen lands. Every day souls are being swept into eternity from these Christian cities, whose parentage was so depraved, whose mental and moral life was so perverted through vicious and brutalized or infidel inheritance, whose poverty was so desperate, whose neighborhood influences were so foul, they never knew enough of the Son of God to make an intelligent rejection of Him. They died, as they had lived, without God and without hope in the world. It is no part of our present duty to speak of the questions raised by what we have just said. To consider

The Rejection of the Atonement

those questions now would be to confuse the issue before us. Whatever our beliefs or our hopes may be concerning the destiny of those who through infancy, disease, or ignorance have been incapable of apprehending on earth the Gospel of the Divine Sacrifice, our reason and our moral sense compel us to see that their relation to God differs not in degree only, but in kind, from that of those who reject the Atonement. Of such are they who have had the Gospel of the Divine Sacrifice fairly presented to their minds, who have intelligently considered it, on its merits, and who reject it by the opposition of the will, whether that opposition be expressed in terms of violent repudiation or in the sustained attitude of calm and steady refusal to acknowledge.

On what authority does the individual venture to speak to his

The Rejection of the Atonement

fellow-men of the nature and the consequences of rejection? Not certainly on the authority of private opinion. That, under the circumstances, were an impertinence. Nor does he speak on the authority of Christian tradition. That, under the circumstances, were but to set one opinion against another. He speaks on the authority which has alone been claimed for all that has hitherto been said, — the authority of the Bible itself as the Word of God.

Upon our findings in that Word an attempt has been made to reason from God's Love as a starting-point up to Jesus Christ and Him crucified, revealed in the Sorrow and Joy of His Sacrifice as the Redeemer of the race. Continuing to report our findings in the Word, it now appears that the Word itself goes far beyond the mere affirmation of the Divine Sacrifice. It

The Rejection of the Atonement

makes knowledge of the Divine Sacrifice a ground of personal responsibility, so that once knowing the fact of the Atonement, the man becomes involved in moral relations toward it from which he cannot escape. The reason for this is that the Gospel of the Divine Sacrifice is an appeal to the man, who having once heard that appeal addressed to himself, must in some manner dispose of it, either by acceptance or by rejection. Christ having offered Himself to the man, the man must, by the necessity of the case, do something with Christ. Every one, believer and unbeliever alike, should therefore, for his own information, fairly confront the proposition of rejecting the Atonement, and should ascertain, not from contemporary human opinion (always tending to local fluctuation), but from the same unaltered source whence comes our knowledge of the Atonement, the

The Rejection of the Atonement

consequences involved in its rejection.

For those who have long lived the life of faith, worshipping Christ as God, and viewing His Sacrifice with sentiments of adoration, gratitude, and affection, it may be difficult to understand the grounds on which one rejects the Atonement. Nevertheless, the rejection of the Atonement is a fact more or less prominent in intellectual life, and as such it is to be reckoned with as we reckon with any other fact observed in human experience. If it transpired that the Atonement were rejected only by the uneducated or by the depraved, we might conclude that education and moral uplift alone are needed to bring one into sympathy with the Cross of Christ. But we find, on the contrary, among those who reject the Atonement minds highly educated, highly philosophical, highly favorable to morality

The Rejection of the Atonement

and religion. If, on the other hand, we found the Atonement to be rejected by all trained and commanding intellects, and accepted only by the lowly and the unlettered, we might conclude that the belief is a survival of superstition, tending to disappear under the growth of knowledge. But we find, instead, many of the noblest minds, leaders of the world's progress, holding a faith that worships Jesus as Divine and regards His Sacrifice as the true ground of peace.

Evidently the causes leading individuals to reject the Atonement must be sought deeper in the consciousness of man. And he who, a believer himself, longs to have others share this noblest of faiths, need not remain in ignorance of those deterring causes, if he will approach his fellow-men in the spirit of sympathetic inquiry rather than in that of wholesale condemnation.

The Rejection of the Atonement

By some cultured minds and generous hearts the Atonement is rejected on grounds of sentiment. There are those who faint at the sight of blood. It is nature's protest against pain and death. Through a corresponding intuition the religious instinct in some rejects with a shudder the death on the Cross. It pronounces the horror of the Crucifixion incompatible with religion. Religion should comfort, uplift, inspire; not horrify the imagination with a vision of streaming blood and deathly anguish. Religion should point man onward to paths of moral excellence, should feed his intellect, should nourish his ambitions; not turn his eyes backward to a far-off scene of misery, nor try to humble his pride before a distant Cross. And so the Passion of Christ is set aside, the Witness of the Bible to the meaning and value of His Sacrifice

The Rejection of the Atonement

is ignored, the relation of God to sin is put from the mind, and sentiment prevailing alike over reason and revelation, soothes itself with soft words of peace.

By some the Atonement is rejected through inertia. Speaking in the language of physical science, inertia is the tendency of a body to continue in its present condition, —if at rest to remain at rest, if in motion to continue in motion. Too readily, under certain conditions, the mind becomes inert; ceases from the constructive energy of urgent thought; wearies of mounting to new planes of knowledge, of climbing to advanced conclusions; submits to stay wherever habit has formed its boundaries; learns to think in grooves; suffers itself to be content with familiar positions. And thus, by some, the rejection of the Atonement occurs by default. It is not a part of the ancestral teach-

The Rejection of the Atonement

ing; it is not one of the familiar ideas; to grasp it demands the constructive energy of fresh thinking; to rise to it calls for the strain and the push of the mountain-climb, up from the beaten track, to higher levels and a keener air. It is too much. Inertia protests. Habit conquers. Christ dies while human minds reject His Atonement by default, through lack of energy to think their way independently to rational conclusions.

By some the Atonement is rejected through a misunderstanding of the Bible's position concerning it. It is not beyond possibility that the Church, in its sincere effort to win souls, may at times have alienated them from the Cross of Christ. Rejection, under such circumstances, would be a double sorrow; a sorrow that one soul should reject, not the Bible doctrine of the Atonement, but some per-

The Rejection of the Atonement

version of the Bible doctrine, taught in all honesty by a zealous Church; a sorrow that the Church, loyal to the Master, and intending to honor Him, should unconsciously so pervert the Gospel of the Divine Sacrifice that it becomes a stumbling block to minds equally loyal to their own ideal of truth, and equally intending to honor God. This mutual misunderstanding is surely the tragedy of faith, a tragedy whose pathos is intensified an hundred-fold because its centre is the Cross of Him Who, in His catholic compassion, tasted death for every man. Yet it is not easy to escape the conviction that some have rejected the Atonement under mistaken opinions of what the Bible doctrine of the Atonement is — and that the Church, in her very zeal for the honor of God, may unhappily have corroborated those opinions. The teaching of a limited

The Rejection of the Atonement

Atonement, or the Death of Christ for only a moiety of the race; and the teaching of what must be described as the vindictive Atonement, or the Death of Christ as a victim to the anger of the Father, may have encouraged some truly devout minds to reject the Divine Sacrifice out of respect for God. The limited Atonement may have been a stumbling-block to faith. A calm review of the history of religious opinions leads one to see that the Gospel of the Christ may have been rejected by some because it was impossible for them to believe that God had deliberately ordained a portion of the race to inevitable salvation, abandoning all others to inevitable damnation; and that Christ had died for the elect only. Such a doctrine of God seemed incompatible with the Morality of His Being, yet as the Church appeared to insist on that doctrine, the

The Rejection of the Atonement

Atonement was set aside, and relief was found in a non-evangelical theism which allowed the mind free expression of its intuitive belief in the love of God. On the other hand, that which we describe as the vindictive Atonement may have been a stumbling-block to faith. When the Church seemed to insist that God the Father was full of rage toward man and was wishing to destroy him, and that Christ the Son, full of love, flung Himself between God and man and permitted the rage to vent itself on Him, so that now a pacified God deigns to love man; there were many who could not endure that conception of God, and rather than submit to it, they refused to grant the Godhead of Christ. They rejected the Atonement as an incredible fiction, and, taking refuge in Unitarianism, they revered Christ as a godlike hero, whilst they worshipped the Love

The Rejection of the Atonement

of God the Father. We shall never know in this world all the spiritual struggle of those who have been compelled to withhold allegiance from the Catholic Faith, and to endure the pain of being looked down upon as unbelievers because they were unable to accept interpretations of the Gospel enforced by ecclesiastical authority. This surely has been the tragedy of faith, all the more pathetic because the Church has been moved to many of her most uncompromising positions by the noblest and purest motives. She taught the limited Atonement that she might exalt the Sovereignty of God; and she taught the Anger of God as appeased in the Blood of Christ because she desired to emphasize the sinfulness of sin. As one thinks of this whole tragedy of faith, one's only confort is in God Himself. If any soul ever rejected the Atonement under an honest mis-

The Rejection of the Atonement

apprehension of its meaning, if any soul ever set the Atonement aside because, as men depicted Christ's Sacrifice, it became a barrier against God instead of a way to God, we know that He to Whom all hearts are open would not judge of one who stumbled before an error, as of one who set his life obstinately against the Truth.

But when these misunderstandings are removed, when the broad doctrine of the Bible opens before us, and we see therein God's Eternal plan of love for the race; sin's catastrophe coming in to oppose the development of that plan, Love proceeding to sweep away by Atonement the barrier in the path of that plan; when we realize that the Bible shows us the Atonement as the act of the Godhead, fulfilled through the Incarnation of one of the Members of the Godhead, Who, out of the pure love of

The Rejection of the Atonement

the Godhead for us, endures humiliation and tastes death, that by the condemnation of sin in His own Person He may satisfy that moral necessity in God's Nature which demands sin's condemnation ere its forgiveness is possible; when the Atonement is seen in Bible light, as the supreme exhibition of a Father's love expressed in the Son, then the situation changes as to a man's responsibility in the rejection of that Atonement. If it be concluded that there may be an intrinsic reasonableness in rejecting the limited Atonement and the vindictive Atonement; that one might reject these interpretations of Christ's Sacrifice out of love and reverence for God, there remains no such reasonableness in the rejection of the Bible Atonement. For the Gospel of the Cross as presented in the Scripture neither antagonizes the intuition of justice, nor affronts

The Rejection of the Atonement

the moral sense. It appeals rather in the highest possible way to our ideals of glory and love. There is nothing to reject, nothing against which to find fault, any more than one may find fault with love for being unselfish. Human instincts accept, acknowledge, and rejoice in love, and the same instincts lead us to accept, to acknowledge, and to rejoice in the Atonement as altogether beautiful and glorious.

When, therefore, after comprehending the Bible doctrine of the Atonement, and seeing it to be such as we have described it to be, a man still rejects God in Christ, there remain two ways of accounting for His rejection of the Atonement. It is rejection because of unbelief, or it is rejection because of resistance to that demand for personal holiness which is included in one's acceptance of the Atonement.

What does one mean by rejection

The Rejection of the Atonement

of the Atonement because of unbelief? Unbelief of what? Unbelief of the Bible as a Revelation, and consequently of those matters revealed in the Bible, — the plan of God's Love, the necessity for sin's condemnation, the condemnation of sin in the Person of Jesus Christ. But one who takes this attitude of unbelief may well be asked to consider the responsibility he assumes in rejecting the Bible Atonement through unbelief of the Bible. He assumes the responsibility of the burden of proof. In disbelieving the Bible one is fairly bound to show cause why the Bible is not credible. In order to defend the position of unbelief one must prove the invalidity and untruthfulness of the Bible. If a man can do this, he is safe and logical in rejecting the Atonement, for the Bible is the only source of testimony to the Fact of the Atonement. But if he cannot

The Rejection of the Atonement

disprove and overthrow the Bible, then he who denies the Bible Atonement (that is, the Atonement as revealed in the Bible) assumes the more serious responsibility of giving the lie to God. "He that believeth not God," says St. John, " hath made Him a liar, because he hath not believed in the witness that God hath borne concerning His Son; and the witness is this, that God gave unto us Eternal Life, and this life is in His Son."

There is another ground on which one can reject the Bible Atonement. Either he does not believe it (which involves the responsibilities just considered) or he does not want it. He rejects it because it calls for personal holiness in those who accept it. The carnal mind is enmity against God. In the last analysis, few perhaps would reject the Atonement, except for that which goes with the Atonement, the call that we shall be

The Rejection of the Atonement

conformed unto Christ's Death by dying to sin in our own hearts and lives. We do not want to have Christ reign over us, not so much because we disbelieve Christ, as because we like to indulge a sinful nature and we hate that crucifixion of self which must become a part of every holy life. One may here be asked to consider what this means, — the rejection of the Atonement because one does not want the crucified Christ to reign over one: a God humiliating Himself for love of man, and a man rejecting the humiliation of His God, because he cares for the evil things on account of which his God was humiliated, more than he cares for his God.

The writer finds it impossible to close this chapter without appealing to any reader who, whether from inertia, or from hostility to ecclesiastical interpretations, or from settled disbelief, may be withholding from the

The Rejection of the Atonement

Gospel of the Cross the allegiance of reason, conscience, and will.

Discriminate between accepting a man's interpretation of the Atonement and believing the Atonement itself. If an interpretation of the Divine Sacrifice can be suggested, better and more Scriptural than that which is stated in the foregoing pages, by all means adopt it. Reject the interpretation if it be unworthy, but let not the rejection of the interpretation include a rejection of the Fact.

The position one assumes in rejecting the Atonement, whether from unbelief or from disinclination for that holier life required of a believer, should be well considered. For by such rejection one thrusts from oneself the only defence against the moral necessity in God's Nature which demands the condemnation of sin; and when we consider what that defence is, even God's interposi-

The Rejection of the Atonement

tion of His own Self, the rejection of the Atonement leaves one the position of not only rejecting the defence, but of insulting the defence, despising the goodness and forbearance of God, and, to use the words of the Bible, "treading under foot the Son of God."

The question that rises in the future before one who rejects deliberately the Bible Atonement should be well considered. The future must be met, and Christ said: "The word that I speak, the same shall judge him in the last day." The question that rises in the future is this: Will God submit to you, or must you submit to God? God's nature requires sin's condemnation. He must condemn. "If we are faithless, He abideth faithful; He cannot deny Himself." Amidst the present interests of our life it is difficult to grasp this thought of the condemnation of sin. Let one

The Rejection of the Atonement

ask oneself, Do I really believe in the condemnation of sin? The condemnation of sin involves the condemnation of persons. Why? Because sin is not something apart from personality; sin is a condition of personality, sin is a state of being. Unless, therefore, one will unite oneself to the Sin-Bearer by a living faith, disowning sin, and, with Christ, dying unto sin, one must bear one's own burden, here and hereafter. Such seems to be the New Testament teaching. The Atonement conceived in the Heart of Godhead, and consummated through the anguish of Christ, cannot be rejected with impunity.

VII

THE PROBLEM OF HUMAN SUFFERING CONSIDERED IN THE LIGHT OF THE DIVINE SACRIFICE

And God saw everything that He had made, and behold, it was very good. BOOK OF GENESIS.

Man that is born of a woman is of few days and full of trouble. He cometh forth like a flower, and is cut down; he fleeth also as a shadow, and continueth not. BOOK OF JOB.

The wages of sin is death, but the free gift of God is Eternal Life in Jesus Christ, our Lord. EPISTLE TO THE ROMANS.

In this was manifested the Love of God towards us, because that God sent His Only Begotten Son into the world that we might live through Him. FIRST EPISTLE OF ST. JOHN.

Blessed be the God and Father of our Lord Jesus Christ, the Father of mercies and God of all comfort, Who comforteth us in all our afflictions, that we may be able to comfort them that are in any affliction, through the comfort wherewith we ourselves are comforted of God. For as the sufferings of Christ abound unto us, even so our comfort also aboundeth through Christ. SECOND EPISTLE TO THE CORINTHIANS.

When we were come into Macedonia our flesh had no relief, but we were afflicted on every side: without were fightings, within were fears. Nevertheless, He That comforteth the lowly, even God, comforted us.
 SECOND EPISTLE TO THE CORINTHIANS.

And I saw a new heaven and a new earth; and God shall wipe away every tear from their eyes; and death shall be no more, neither shall there be mourning nor crying nor pain any more; the first things are passed away. And He That sitteth on the Throne said: Behold, I make all things new.
 THE REVELATION OF ST. JOHN THE DIVINE.

Chapter VII

The Problem of Human Suffering considered in the Light of the Divine Sacrifice

No one who reflects upon the intricacy and the mystery of all life is surprised to find dark problems surrounding the condition and the destiny of man. The absence of such problems would be a greater mystery than their presence. Man's finiteness broadens out on every side toward God's infiniteness, and life's mystery is also life's majesty.

One of the darkest problems surrounding the condition of man is the problem of Human Suffering. Disappointment, unrest, sorrow, sickness, trouble, death, are everywhere. Wherever man goes, suffering goes,

Suffering and Sacrifice

lying, as it were, in ambush for him. It matters not what man's errand may be, the best or the worst, suffering awaits him. He may go out into life as the teacher, the comforter, the missionary, the friend,— or he may go as the destroyer, the robber, the seducer, the knave — go how he will, and for what he will, he suffers, he sorrows, he dies. Such is the omnipresence of human suffering, of this dark enigma of sorrow. One may say of it as the Psalmist said of God: "Whither shall I flee from Thy presence? If I take the wings of the morning and dwell in the uttermost parts of the sea, even there shall Thy hand lead me. If I say, Surely the darkness shall cover me, the darkness hideth not from Thee, the darkness and the light are both alike to Thee." Who can travel so far, who can protect himself so thoroughly, who can seclude himself so profoundly that he

Suffering and Sacrifice

shall escape from trouble and sorrow and pain and death?

That man forever attempts to solve this dark problem of human suffering, to give some rational account of this stern condition inseparable from his life, is the result of an original intuition of man's nature. Involuntarily we tend to trace all sensations to their source. Walking in spring-time through some hollow lane of Devonshire, we catch the waft of violets, and lift the eyes to note the bank, purple with bloom. Standing in sunlight we see a shadowed form outlined on the path beside our own, and turn to identify the friend who has joined us. Tortured with some strange pain shooting through the head or clutching at the heart, we go to the physician to learn what lesion is its cause. This is intuitive inquiry into the causes of sensations. And the same intuition prompts man to solve

Suffering and Sacrifice

the problem of the universal human sorrow. It is incredible that rational beings involved in suffering shall not try to find out why they suffer.

Invariably when man confronts the problem of suffering he uses his doctrine of God to aid him in the solution. The history of human thought in all times and in all religions will, it is believed, be found to verify this statement. By a companion intuition to that which prompts man to ask why he suffers, man is prompted to feel that God is in some way related to his sufferings. This would be true in the case of an atheist, if there exists such a state of mind as pure atheism. The atheist, denying the existence of God, would thereby relate the conception of a God negatively to human suffering, saying: " There being no God, the God-idea has no bearing whatever on the sufferings

Suffering and Sacrifice

of the human race." This would be true in the case of the agnostic, who declines to commit himself to a positive statement of belief on the subject of God. He would relate God tentatively to human trouble, saying: "He may send it, or He may not; in the absence of physical demonstration it is impossible to tell." This would be true in the case of the ethnic religions; for example, in the case of Zoroastrianism, the ancient Persian faith, with its dualism, — two co-eternal gods, arrayed against one another in ceaseless opposition touching man's condition. There is Ormuzd, the god of good, sending every blessing on the race; there is Ahriman, the god of evil, showering upon humanity woe, disappointment, and every form of ill. These illustrations might be indefinitely multiplied, and in each case we would discover the tendency of the human mind to place a doctrine

Suffering and Sacrifice

of God in some relation, negative, tentative, or positive, to the problem of suffering. The reason for this is plain; the sufferings of the race are so tremendous, so unceasing, and in innumerable instances so out of proportion to any recognized standard of justice, there is a feeling too deep for analysis, too axiomatic to call for demonstration, that in some way, if there is a God, humanity's one hope of present consolation or of future relief must connect itself with Him, and be evolved through Him. Deep down below all creeds, the hope of a suffering world utters that many-sided, infinite syllable "God," and feeling the problem of suffering to be greater than man can handle alone, confesses, sometimes scarce knowing what it means: "To whom shall we go but unto Thee!"

When we confine our thought to our own religion, and ask in what manner believers in Christianity have

Suffering and Sacrifice

brought the doctrine of God to bear upon the problem of human suffering, we behold rising before us that tremendous and venerable conception of an Infinite One, Whose right no one may dispute, Who has foreordained whatsoever comes to pass, Whose Hand is in all things, Who for His own glory, and in the exercise of His own sovereignty, has sent and will send whatever comes to man. As the mighty peak of Teneriffe rises in imperial majesty out of the Southern Ocean, and sweeps upward twelve thousand feet into the glittering sunshine, ancient, motionless, solid, symmetrical, silent, sharp, white, barren; while around it on every hand stretches the waste of the troubled sea, with the swelling of its tides, and the moaning of its surge, and the ghastly secrets of its depths, and the interminable uplift of short-lived billows, rising in momentary light, to sink again in

Suffering and Sacrifice

darkness,—so rises this metaphysical conception of the imperial sovereignty of God into the highest air of abstract thought, in infinite self-removal from the actual level of the world's experience and the world's intuitive sense of need. Behold it, poised in glittering majesty, a conception of God, ancient, motionless, solid, symmetrical, silent, sharp, barren, a peak of thought, standing alone, the solitary goal of a few explorers; a God who, from His eagle eyrie, looks down on a world where all things happen as they were ordained, where evil that might be stopped is infinitely permitted, and sorrow that might be spared is infinitely sent. The troubled sea of human lives moans and heaves about that silent peak of God; millions of lives, like waves, lift themselves up toward it in momentary hope, and sink away into the mass; and deep in the heart of the sea of human life

Suffering and Sacrifice

are secrets of death which no sunlight ever reaches, no tide ever sweeps away, no voice from the barren peak ever explains.

It may seem both idle and presumptuous for one man to question that ancient and deep-seated conception of God's relation to human suffering, as if one were to stand before the peak of Teneriffe and say, " Be thou removed, and be thou cast into the sea." Nevertheless, a man's faith has Christ's guarantee, even when it attempts to remove mountains. But if that mountain were never removed, if the prevailing belief of Christians were to continue to be what it has so long been, it is, not a right only, but a duty, to show how one who loves and reverences the Bible as Divine may start with the pure and simple teachings of that Word and reach conclusions as far removed from those just described as the lofty head

Suffering and Sacrifice

of Teneriffe is from the moaning, restless waves that fling themselves eternally against its base. Far be it from the writer to question any man's right so to relate God to the problem of human suffering as may best relieve the pressure of that problem upon his own mind. It is well if through such a belief as has just been depicted any who suffer are being comforted; but there are other possible conclusions concerning God's relation to suffering, which appear when, as now, an attempt is made to consider that problem in the light of the Divine Sacrifice.

Those who have followed the argument through the six preceding chapters will perceive the bearing upon the subject of human suffering of what has been said about the causes and conditions of Christ's sufferings. We are conducted to our present theme by the tendency

Suffering and Sacrifice

of our previous reasonings. Comprehensive thought upon the Divine Sacrifice must lead the mind ultimately to consider God's relation to human suffering in the light of that Sacrifice. Furthermore, intuition prompts us, as we have already remarked, to bring our doctrine of God to bear upon our doctrine of suffering, in the hope that the glory and the joy of the one may relieve the gloom and the stress of the other.

The belief that God sends trouble, that the calamities and miseries, the pangs, losses, and death of the children of men are in a mysterious way according to His Will, is a belief repugnant to our natural sensibilities. It can only be held, in connection with love toward God, by the aid of a strong and submissive faith, inasmuch as it violates our instinctive conception of what love will do. The belief that a

Suffering and Sacrifice

God of perfect love and tenderness is causing directly or by indirection the grievous sufferings of the human race, and is daily adding to the sum of sorrow many thousands of freshly afflicted hearts, can be sincerely embraced only by an heroic effort of faith holding in check our natural inclinations to the contrary view. Yet beyond question multitudes have succeeded in this effort of faith, and have loved God while looking upon Him as the sender of their trouble. Some of the most impressive and majestic exhibitions of the loyalty of faith ever witnessed have come from saintly souls, quivering with the anguish of earthly sorrows, yet looking in their agony up to God, as the One Who sent the bereavement, or the maiming, or the disgrace, or the sudden poverty; and taking the blow without a murmur, supposing it to be a just rebuke administered by Himself. An ex-

Suffering and Sacrifice

planation of this phenomenon, of a religion that develops a doctrine of God in antagonism to those intuitions of God which He has implanted in us, may perhaps be found in that form of stating the doctrine of God's Sovereignty which has prevailed since a very early time. To the peculiarities of this form of statement we have referred at length in earlier chapters. Its two most important peculiarities are these: that the anger of God against man has only been appeased by the bloody Sacrifice of the innocent Christ: that by a decree of election which determines destiny, and by a limited Atonement, God has reserved a portion of the race unto an inevitable salvation, leaving the remainder of the race unto an equally inevitable damnation.

These are leading ideas in that ancient mode of stating the Divine Sovereignity which has prevailed cen-

Suffering and Sacrifice

tury after century, often accompanied with extreme intonations of fierceness and threatening. Generation after generation has been told by its teachers that God is angry with man, and was on the point of eternally damning man, when Christ, the heroic, innocent Sufferer, interposed, and by His freely given blood, slaked the fierceness of the wrath of God. Generation after generation has been told by its teachers that God, for the purpose of demonstrating His Sovereignty, singles out some by a decree unto life, abandoning all others unto endless hell; and that Christ died not for all men, but for the moiety of the race predestined unto life. These teachings, urged continuously and solemnly upon successive generations, and handed down reverently from fathers to children, become not only the substantial and unquestioned substance and fibre of faith,

Suffering and Sacrifice

but develop necessarily just such a doctrine of sorrow as we find to be so widely and so submissively held: that all things are from God, that evil not positively sent is negatively permitted, amounting thereby to the same thing; that woes and miseries, as well as all other human experiences, are parts of His Will, and in accordance with His Plan under that eternal decree which, from before the foundation of the world, necessitated all that is. This is the reasonable conclusion from the existing premises; and the fact that man is God's child and made for God, and that man cannot live without God, is nowhere more marvellously shown than in the magnificent loyalty with which suffering souls have clung to God in the face of a doctrine of God's Sovereignty which teaches them that He is raining the blows of trouble upon them.

Suffering and Sacrifice

The writer distinctly disavows all intention and desire to oppose the views just indicated, and the venerated Confession upon which they are founded. On the contrary, he regards that Confession as a sacred monument of the Christian Faith, honored of God throughout many generations.

But for the sake of those who cannot accept this mode of stating the Sovereignty of God, and who, rather than believe it, would turn from God and wander out into the darkness of agnosticism, staggering under life's intolerable weight of trouble, it is the reverent and humble purpose of this book to suggest *an alternate* doctrine of God, which leads to *an alternate* doctrine of sorrow, when the problem of human suffering is viewed in the light of the Divine Sacrifice. The starting-point of all our thought in this matter is that the Atonement is not the cause of God's Love, but

Suffering and Sacrifice

that God's Love is the cause of the Atonement. God's eternal attitude toward man is Love, the love of a father for his child. This love was formulated in God's Mind before the foundation of the world, in that Plan for a beloved race that we should be conformed to the Image of His Son. Into the world came man; godlike, beautiful, holy; wearing, as the very diadem of individuality, the inalienable power of choice. And God saw all that He had made, and behold it was very good. To man in his splendid innocency and in his godlike freedom came the tempter, himself the outcome of a moral tragedy older than man, and, working on the unfallen will of the new race, with arts and influences second only to the power of God Himself, the tempter drew the human will into choices contrary to the Will of God. Thus entered sin, the principle of disorganization, con-

Suffering and Sacrifice

fusion, and catastrophe; blighting, weakening, cursing all life everywhere; working out, under the perpetual misuses of law, the infinitudes of sorrow, pain, disease, weariness, death. How soon had the scene changed! Out of the prehistoric book of Job comes the grievous lament over a fallen race: "Man that is born of a woman is of few days and full of misery. He cometh up as a flower, and is cut down. He fleeth also as a shadow, and continueth not."

The Heart of God was full of grief as His beloved ones demeaned themselves in His Presence, and spurned their birthright before His Face. Yet in His Heart never failed nor wavered that great Plan of love for humanity. He yearned to forgive and to restore. Yet forgiveness and restoration could not come without sacrifice; for the moral necessity of His own Nature demanded the con-

Suffering and Sacrifice

demnation of sin ere it could be forgiven. He could not be indifferent to sin; He could not consent to sin; He must, by the moral necessity of His own Nature, condemn sin as an intolerable condition in the universe, an intolerable interruption of His Plan for the beloved race. And the Atonement is the means devised by Divine Love to meet the moral necessity of Divine Holiness. The Atonement is the act of the Godhead. Christ is God in the flesh of man, and as a Member of the Godhead, enduring the condemnation of sin in His own Person as the Representative of the race; offering His Sacrifice for the whole world without respect of persons, and so satisfying the demand of God's Holiness that sin be condemned ere sin can be forgiven. We have pondered both the Sorrow and the Joy of Christ in His Sacrifice. We have seen His Sorrow, as He viewed sin's hideous

Suffering and Sacrifice

consequences in human life, and, with Divine hatred of sin, condemned it as the devilish cause of human woe, and the devilish impediment in the path of God's illustrious Plan of love for the race. We have seen His Joy, as He felt Himself, through His own sufferings and humiliations, brought into closest fellowship with all human suffering, and into deepest comprehension of all human need. He looked from the eminence of His Cross to the far-reaching results of His Sacrifice: the furtherance of God's eternal Plan for the glory and happiness of man; the reconstruction of human society on a new basis of sympathy, purity, and aspiration; the ultimate victory of light over darkness, of joy over sorrow, of good over evil; the coming of a millennial kingdom, when the vestiges of the old catastrophe of sin and death shall at last be done away for all who are united

Suffering and Sacrifice

to Himself, and when for them there shall be death no more, neither sorrow, nor crying, nor pain, and God shall wipe away all tears from their eyes.

This is our alternate doctrine of God. Thus, assuming the Inspiration of Scripture and the Godhead of Christ, we interpret the Gospel of the Divine Sacrifice, self-consistent in the eternal past, in the mysterious present, in the glorious future: Jesus Christ, the same yesterday, to-day, and forever; revealing God as the Lover of man, the Sacrifice for man, the Redeemer of man, the Comforter of man, the Restorer to man, at last, of that long-lost birthright of power and peace, marred through many generations by sin and sorrow.

In the light of this Divine Sacrifice we now view the problem of human suffering; and lo! the conditions of that problem are wondrously altered. The suffering

Suffering and Sacrifice

is the same, but the problem is changed. The darkest enigma hovering over human suffering vanishes when we believe that all is as it is, not because God wills it, but because the blessed Plan He willed for the world is thrust aside by man's perversity. The trouble that in a thousand forms fills the world to-day is the melancholy harvest of generations of weakening tendencies, mistaken ideas, sinful propensities, and foolish choices, complicated by the added errors of each new day of life. Awful as that harvest is, one can yet look upon it without despair in the light of the Divine Sacrifice. For the Face that we see upon the Cross is not the face of him that wrought this confusion and wreaked this misery; it is not the face of the enemy that sowed the tares of evil amid the wheat of good; it is the Face of Him Who loved us and gave Himself up for

Suffering and Sacrifice

us; the Face of Him Who, forasmuch as the children of men were partakers of flesh and blood, Himself also took part of the same, that through death He might destroy him that hath the power of death, that is, the devil; the Face of Him Who bore our griefs and carried our sorrows; the Face of Him That sitteth on the Throne and saith: "Behold, I make all things new." And as we look upon that wondrous Face, marred then with sorrow, radiant now with victory, we attribute not to Him any share in causing the sufferings of the race for which He died; we soil not the lustre of His Name by involving it with distresses which are, directly or indirectly, the outcome of our sinful estate. "The wages of sin is death, but the free gift of God is eternal life, through Jesus Christ our Lord."

Does God send trouble? Fear not to ask and to answer that ques-

Suffering and Sacrifice

tion when you confront the dark mystery of human suffering. But ask it and answer it in the light of the Divine Sacrifice. Answer it not in the presence of those startling acts of judgment recorded in the Old Testament Annals, lest you be drawn by local conditions far out of touch with God's essential relation to man. Those Old Testament acts of judgment were the heroic measures by which He roused to moral consciousness His beloved race when it had sunk to that abyss of degradation of which St. Paul speaks in the first chapter of Romans, when the very sense of right and wrong had vanished into insensibility, and could only be resuscitated through shocks of judgment. Take not those peculiar conditions as your standard of inquiry in answering the question, Does God send trouble? And answer not that question by observations made along the

Suffering and Sacrifice

narrow groove of your personal affairs, lest the snare of a perverted doctrine of Providence capture you, and you conceive of troubles and worries springing from evident physical causes as petty persecutions from God to drive you into the way of righteousness. Ask the question, Does God send trouble? as you stand before the Cross of Jesus Christ, as you worship Him in His Godhead, as you realize that His Humiliation is the supreme expression of God's hatred for sin, as disobedience in its essence and as sorrow and misery in its results; ask it at the Cross, and an answer will be given you out of the depths of the Divine Sacrifice, to make you sure that He Who died to redeem the race is not he who by trouble and sorrow is making men old before their time, and breaking women down with hardship and anguish.

Suffering and Sacrifice

But when you have asked and answered that question, Does God send trouble? ask and answer another, — that you may have peace in your soul toward God, — even this: Does God permit trouble? Surely he who permits the evil he might avert does not remove himself far in our thought from him who sends the evil. Fear not to ask, then, even this question in the light of the Divine Sacrifice: Does He permit the evil and trouble which are riding rough-shod over human lives to-day? To permit! What is it to permit? It is to consent to, to grant license or liberty to do. And must we stand before the Cross of Jesus Christ, knowing that the sorrows of the world are directly or indirectly the wages and fruits of sin, and say that God gives His consent to these sorrows and troubles by licensing the causes that produce them? Say it if you must.

Suffering and Sacrifice

Many saintly souls have said it, and say it to-day. Some cannot say it. For them, is there not another answer, even this, to the question, Does God permit trouble? No! He is against it as He is against the causes from which it springs. Why then does it exist? Because man is free, and his freedom is the one thing God cannot take away from him. He gave him the freedom of his volition as an inalienable and constitutional gift, when He gave him his being; and it is man's misuse of his freedom that makes this world a world of sorrow. It cannot be otherwise until man is subdued in his will to God. It cannot be otherwise until each member of the redeemed race shall have consecrated his personal will to Him Who gave it. For those who may never do this, there remains the eternal possibility of producing trouble and sorrow; this possibility makes hell on

Suffering and Sacrifice

earth, and while this possibility remains, if earth were blotted out, hell would still be left. For those whose wills are given to God, at last there shall be deliverance from all evil,—not on earth, but afterward,—where there cannot enter aught that defileth or maketh a lie; where the limitations of earth are left behind; where the eyes of the blind are opened, and the feet of the lame are healed; where the inhabitant shall no more say "I am sick;" where death shall be no more; where there shall be neither mourning nor crying nor pain any more; where the wicked cease from troubling, and the weary are at rest; where God is seen at length in His Beauty, that Perfect Beauty of Perfect Love, which, on earth, we were sometimes slow of heart to believe.

VIII

THE SOVEREIGNTY OF GOD

And I heard as it were the voice of a great multitude, and as the voice of many waters, and as the voice of mighty thunderings, saying: "Alleluia, for the Lord God Omnipotent reigneth. Let us be glad and rejoice, and give honor to Him.

THE REVELATION OF ST. JOHN THE DIVINE.

Thou hast put all things in subjection under His Feet. For in that He put all in subjection under Him, He left nothing that is not put under Him. But now we see not all things put under Him.

EPISTLE TO THE HEBREWS.

For He must reign till He hath put all His enemies under His Feet. The last enemy that shall be abolished is death. For He put all things in subjection under His Feet.

FIRST EPISTLE TO THE CORINTHIANS.

Chapter VIII

The Sovereignty of God

FROM all the many Scriptures which dwell on the Sovereignty of God, it would be difficult to select one more splendidly representative than that from the Vision of St. John in which he declares: "And I heard as it were the voice of a great multitude, and as the voice of many waters, and as the voice of mighty thunderings, saying: Alleluia, for the Lord God Omnipotent reigneth. Let us be glad and rejoice and give honor to Him." This is a prophecy of the celestial Te Deum, of that final and most mighty canticle which shall ring through eternity when God is truly seen and truly understood by the

The Sovereignty of God

mind of man. This New Testament prophecy is Humanity's acknowledgment of God's Sovereignty — not God's proclamation of it, but Humanity's voluntary acknowledgment of it. Man is to pour out alleluias in Heaven because an Omnipotent God is on the Throne.

The spontaneous popular acknowledgment of sovereignty is, even to a republican mind, an impressive and thought-awakening spectacle. Some never read these words of St. John about the voice of the great multitude like the voice of many waters and of mighty thunderings, without recalling the hour in which they saw Queen Victoria proceed to the Abbey to give thanks to God for fifty years of sovereignty. Four millions of her subjects lined the route of that stately procession. Not a note of martial music stirred the air as the earthly sovereign went

The Sovereignty of God

in silence to bow before the King of kings; but as she came along the way, from afar her coming was heralded by a sound the like of which one may not expect to hear twice in a lifetime. It was the shoutings and applaudings of millions; and as that strange, unearthly torrent of sound swept down the gorgeous highway, beneath a thousand banners fluttering from the red Venetian masts, one could without irreverence think of it as a type of St. John's great vision of Humanity's final acknowledgment of the Sovereignty of God, the spontaneous testimony of consenting voices, like the surf of oceans, or thunders from the purple cloud: "Alleluia, for the Lord God Omnipotent reigneth."

St. John's Vision is also the acknowledgment of God's Sovereignty by man at the highest stage of human development. This is the heavenly Alleluia; man's highest

The Sovereignty of God

view of God. It is a declaration that man's belief in God's Sovereignty is not the product of ignorance and superstition; not an idea of the Dark Ages, a glorious fable fading out into the light of common day as science advances and as physical laws are better understood; but rather that this thought of the reign of an Omnipotent God, a thought as old as humanity, is confirmed by every advance of knowledge, is strengthened in the consciousness of each succeeding age, as the race ascends toward its final destiny; and becomes in heaven, where man is at his best, the foundation of the highest thought and the confession of the final faith. The Sovereignty of God is the Creed of Glorified Humanity: " Alleluia, for the Lord God Omnipotent reigneth."

St. John's Vision is also the acknowledgment of God's Sovereignty when earth's confused story shall be

The Sovereignty of God

ended, and when humanity shall look back upon the earth-history from the vantage-point of a superior state of being. Earth's history has been such an inextricable web of confusion from the beginning, such a chaos of evil and good, of hideousness and holiness, of barbarity and blessedness, men have had many minds about the power of God. Some have swung to the atheistic extreme, and have said in their hearts: There is no God. Some have swung to the fatalistic extreme, and have said: There is nothing but God, for all that comes to pass in the earth of every sort is the Will of God the Sovereign. Some have stood between the two extremes, hesitant or stupefied in the presence of life's colossal contradictions, not knowing what to believe, what to disbelieve; afraid of faith, and equally afraid of doubt. But one rejoices in the Vision of St. John as

The Sovereignty of God

an aid to faith, in that it shows a view of God which shall ultimately prevail in the mind of man. When man shall reach the point in the future whence he can look back on what now seems to him the utterly confused history of time; when he shall read, not one torn fragment of a page in the great book of humanity's world-chronicle, but the whole vast tome from cover to cover; when "earth breaks up and heaven expands," and man's intelligence studies God with eyes no longer dimmed by tears and blurred by mists, — the Sovereignty of God shall be acknowledged with an unanimity that shall sound before the Throne like the break of waves and the peal of thunder. "Alleluia, for the Lord God Omnipotent reigneth!"

And yet once more: this is not only the acknowledgment of the Sovereignty, but the acknowledgment that the Sovereignty is a

The Sovereignty of God

reason for gladness and rejoicing; that the Sovereignty of God is not tyranny, not cold, impenetrable fate, not the Kismet of Islam, beneath which conduct becomes submission to the inevitable; but a Sovereignty that stimulates to love and happiness and worship, that fills heaven with delight, and eternity with freedom. " Alleluia, for the Lord God Omnipotent reigneth. Let us be glad and rejoice, and give honor to him." Thus does St. John's Vision reveal a conception of the Sovereignty of God upon which every mind can look with delight.

Undoubtedly the Sovereignty of God is one of the root ideas of our religion, and of that Hebrew faith which is, chronologically, the parent stock of Christianity. The infiniteness of the Power of God, His eternal and inalienable seat upon His Throne, His authority over all things, visible and invisible, is at

The Sovereignty of God

the very foundation of worship. And nowhere in Scripture is God's Sovereignty more impressively proclaimed than in the contrasts drawn again and again between the august dignity of Theism and the pathetic attempts of idolatry to set up for worship man-made creations that fail at every point to satisfy the hopes of those who trust in them. The scene on Carmel between Elijah and the Baal worshippers is immortal for the tragic contrast drawn between the Sovereign Jehovah and the impotent Baal; and where will one find anything more magnificent than the march of thought in the 115th Psalm, where Theism is set off against idolatry: " Wherefore should the nations say: where is now their God? Our God is in the heavens; He hath done whatsoever He pleased. Their idols are silver and gold; the work of men's hands. They have mouths, but they

The Sovereignty of God

speak not; eyes have they, but they see not; they have ears, but they hear not; noses have they, but they smell not; they have hands, but they handle not; feet have they, but they walk not; neither speak they through their throat. They that make them shall be like unto them. Yea, every one that trusteth in them. O'Israel, trust thou in the Lord; He is their help and their shield."

One may say with truth, there is no discussion, among those who believe the Bible, as to the Sovereignty of God. That is both assumed and expressed in all Christian thought. Upon that Rock we build the entire structure of our faith. He who assails the Sovereignty of God assails not only our religion, but the great presupposition on which religion stands. Shatter or even shake that Rock-Thought of God's Sovereignty, and our religion, built on it, collapses like a flimsy tenement.

The Sovereignty of God

But while belief in the Sovereignty of God is unanimous and unquestioned, there are differences in the interpretation of that fact, differences of view as to the manner in which God exercises His Sovereignty. The minds of men, by reason of temperament, training, and others influences, study the Sovereignty from different points of view, and report differently concerning its mode, while agreeing absolutely in the fact. The Sovereignty of God is regarded as a fact wherever Christian thought prevails, but the point of view from which one sets out to study the Bible doctrine of God may lead to conclusions regarding the mode in which Sovereignty is exercised which are different from those entertained by him who has thought his way to God along another line of ideas. Each should do full justice to the fairness and consecration of the

The Sovereignty of God

other. Each should think less of the differences in individual points of view than of the oneness of the all-important fact, which both are contemplating and which enables both alike to say: " Alleluia, for the Lord God Omnipotent reigneth."

The main difference between interpretations of the mode of God's Sovereignty lies at one point, namely, this: There are those who, starting with the idea of the eternal decree fixing in advance the destiny of each individual in the life hereafter, reason with relation to the present life that everything in this life must also be fixed by the decree, and that the Sovereignty of God consists in His absolute control over all that is, so that nothing comes to pass save as an expression, direct or indirect, of His Omnipotent Will. On the other hand, there are those who cannot accept that interpretation of Scripture which represents God as

The Sovereignty of God

fixing in advance by a decree the destiny of His creatures in a future life, and such minds, reasoning with relation to the present life, see no necessity that events in our present state of being shall be fixed by a decree. It seems to them that the Sovereignty of God stands in more harmonious relation to the other attributes of His Character, such as Love, and Justice, and Truth, and is greatly exalted and glorified when it is regarded as carrying forward an eternal Plan of Love, notwithstanding those adverse conditions which prevail by reason of sin; and is not looked upon as bringing to pass all that takes place in a world where, apparently, sin, and injustice, and dishonor, and cruelty, and mistake have a large influence in producing the conditions which we find to exist.

It is assumed that the reader is familiar with the two interpretations

The Sovereignty of God

of the idea of God's Sovereignty here briefly delineated. The former of the two theories, that which attributes every event directly or indirectly to the Sovereignty of God, could not perhaps be better summed up, in its essential intent, than by quoting the familiar saying, "Whatever is, is right." The writer yields to no one in his admiration for some who have gone through life, and for some who are now valiantly going through life, with this as their motto. He appreciates the unflinching loyalty which prompts a man or a woman in the presence of that which by every instinct of nature, and by every impulse of morality, one inclines to pronounce bad and wrong, and cruel and infamous, still to say, "Whatever is, is right." That which makes such a position possible — and it is possible for many — is the interpretation put upon the Sovereignty of God; namely, that

The Sovereignty of God

the Sovereignty of God is impaired if anything takes place contrary to His Will; that if we grant the occurrence of events in which God has had no part, we make the Devil greater than God, and take from the very brow of Infinity its crown of Sovereignty. If this interpretation of Sovereignty be the only one consistent with Scripture, let us bow to it, and in time learn, from the example of some whose characters we revere, to bow to it without a murmur. For we cannot part with our belief in God's Sovereignty without parting with our religion; and if it must be that the Sovereignty of God cannot be maintained on other grounds, then we will take it on this ground; we will bow to the inevitable; we will even say " Kismet " with the Mohammedan; for we cannot live without God, and a God there cannot be without Sovereignty. The universe is void of Deity, unless " the Lord God

The Sovereignty of God

Omnipotent reigneth." A God without Sovereignty is no God.

It is fair to state why some have felt that this conception of an absolute sovereignty controlling all events, good and bad, and bringing to pass all that is, is not the highest and most magnificent conception of God's Sovereignty which the mind is capable of entertaining. It may be pointed out, in passing, that the general tendency of an advancing Christian civilization is to modify and soften and restrain the more extreme views of sovereignty which prevailed in an earlier and less intelligent age. The sovereign of a barbaric or semi-barbaric state identifies with his sovereignty, not only as its right, but as a condition of its existence, the freedom to do anything, good or bad. The sovereignty of the semi-barbaric state is absolutism. A fair example of it is seen to-day at Constantinople,

The Sovereignty of God

in the person of a Sultan issuing in one breath rigid instructions for the safety of resident foreigners, and in the next mowing down helpless women and children with the dripping scimitars of Kurdish tribesmen. An advanced Christian civilization knows that true sovereignty needs no such absolutism wherewith to maintain itself; that sovereignty reaches its highest dignity when, self-limited by the restraints of righteousness and mercy, it works for the larger good in the uplifting of men and the peace of nations. So also it appears to some that the Sovereignty of God needs no such support as that theory of absolutism which would set God behind all the events of the world, the indiscriminate Providence, dealing misery as well as happiness, confusion as well as peace, profligacy as well as piety, disease as well as health. Some question if there be not a loftier concep-

The Sovereignty of God

tion of a Divine Sovereignty than this, even as there is a loftier conception of human sovereignty than that which corresponds to this. But still further, we question whether the Bible does not directly and continuously say that God is not in everything, and that the world is passing through experiences in which many vast forces are at work which in no sense represent Christ, but Anti-Christ,— that which is against God and contrary to God. We question whether the Bible does not directly state that the Sovereignty of God is not now supreme on earth. If it were supreme now, if whatever is, is right, for what could even God ask beyond this? But does not the Bible say that God's Sovereignty is not now supremely effective over all life, that there are enemies yet to be subdued, and that it is to be supreme in the end? Does not the Bible say: " Thou hast put all things in subjec-

The Sovereignty of God

tion under His Feet. For in that He put all in subjection under Him, He left nothing that is not put under Him. But now we see not yet all things put under Him. For He must reign till He hath put all His enemies under His Feet. The last enemy that shall be abolished is death." It thus appears that God's Sovereignty needs no such support as that which those devout men have sought to give who have held that we make the devil greater than God unless we regard all events as issuing from the One Almighty Source. What, then, is that interpretation of the Sovereignty of God which, in the belief of some, rises to a higher plane of thought and leads the worshipper up to a grander view of the Divine Majesty?

Some features of this other interpretation may be stated. They are stated tentatively. Some may adopt them with the full consent of reason,

The Sovereignty of God

affection, faith, and will; daring to take, not one step alone, but all the steps that lead the mind from the Sovereignty of God in the eternal past, to His Sovereignty in the earthly present; and on to that glorious outlook in the eternal future, when all things shall be subdued unto Him, and when God shall be all in all. For those who can take these steps, the Sovereignty of God becomes a thought of enrapturing joy; and even here, in the struggle of the earth, one seems by anticipation to take one's part in that great canticle of the glorified: " Alleluia, for the Lord God Omnipotent reigneth."

The Sovereignty of God is seen in that Infinite Plan concerning man, conceived in the eternal past by the Mind of the Omnipotent. Before the foundations of the world were laid, there lay in the Infinite Mind a Purpose to make a race of beings

The Sovereignty of God

peculiarly identified with Himself in nature, and susceptible of development into ideal perfection, according to the perfection of the Christ-Image.

The Sovereignty of God is seen in the existence of man. That the creature on whom the Infinite Mind pondered in Eternity came to exist in time, is an act of Sovereignty. Whatever theory of human origins may at last prevail, the fact antedates all theories concerning it. Man exists. He finds himself upon the earth. The Creator has created what the Sovereign has willed.

The Sovereignty of God is seen in the freedom of man. Freedom is the crowning endowment of the man. That man shall be free like God, was the Plan. That man is free, is the sovereign act of Him Who planned. This freedom is freedom, not the burlesque and pantomime of freedom. This freedom implies the power to sin. Short-sighted,

The Sovereignty of God

we cry "Oh, why does God make man with the power to sin?" Ah! look further on before you answer; look on into the future; remember that the power to sin implies also the power not to sin, and the Plan of the Eternal shall not be consummated until this race of beings having the power to sin, and 'for a time using that power perversely, shall reach at length the Godward use of freedom in perfect union with the Plan of their Sovereign.

The Sovereignty of God is seen in the unaltered constitution of law, notwithstanding man's long misuse of freedom. The world was a perfect world; and the world is a perfect world to-day, in its organic structure and law. And as at the beginning man found that certain uses of his freedom contrary to the Divine order of the world would bring, in the nature of the case, certain results unfavorable to health and happiness,

The Sovereignty of God

so he finds that the Divine order of the world is unchanged to-day, and whoever resists it, sooner or later breaks himself against it. But the confusion and the sorrow are a million times increased and complicated, and the innocent are helplessly involved with the guilty by the persistence of the race in its misuses of freedom. Man listens to the evil and impure spirit when he should listen to the Holy and Divine Spirit. He resists the Sovereignty of God, and breaks himself and others to pieces against the Divine order of a great and glorious world.

The Sovereignty of God is seen in the persistence of His Plan of Love, notwithstanding the presence of evil and the activity of Satanic influence. Can any one ask if we are making God less than the devil when one looks back upon the stupendous progress of the Plan of

The Sovereignty of God

God through the ages of history? With sin a constant possibility, growing out of the very existence of human and angelic freedom; with sin a fearful fact from the beginning; with human perversity and devilish malignity growing more intense at every point, — what has the Sovereign done, what is He doing, for the race He loves? Let Christ and Christianity be the answer: The Divine Sacrifice and the Universal Gospel. History is the answer to those who think that God is put beneath Satan, when we cease to count God the Author of events which are incompatible with His Character. The victories of truth, the growth of liberty, the triumphs of Christ's Gospel, the Mission of the Holy Ghost since Pentecost, tell us that He Who once in the lonely wilderness cried, " Get Thee behind Me, Satan," is the Sovereign Who is grandly working out His Plan

The Sovereignty of God

under conditions adapted in all respects to the inherent and inalienable freedom of the race.

The Sovereignty of God is seen in His constant uses of evil for the education of the race and of the individual. He Who made a sinless race with power to live in untainted blessedness, and with power to plunge itself in misery, when that race takes the weaker course and plunges itself in misery, shows His Sovereignty in no more marvellous way than in His power to overrule mistakes and calamities and sins, so that out of their misery may come consequences that shall help toward the redemption of the race. So Saul is converted by impressions received at the bloody death of Stephen; so countless inventions and discoveries, of infinite consolation and help to the afflicted race, have sprung out of conditions wholly produced by sin and misery. The hideousness of

The Sovereignty of God

disease has stimulated the power and enriched the resources of surgery, and above all else, the Holy Spirit, dealing with Christians plunged in human misery, has brought out spiritual results of patience, heroism, holy consecration which have made the name of "saint" the highest and greatest title a human life can bear.

The Sovereignty of God is seen in that Vision of the Final Triumph, when the Plan that was conceived in the eternal past shall have reached, through and over all hindrances perversely thrust in its way, by the freedom of fallen men and devils, that only consummation which is possible under the Omnipotence of God. Satan's power shall be checked and chained. Sin, and those who persist in it, shall no more hinder the onward sweep of an Omnipotent Purpose. Death shall be swallowed up in victory; sorrow and sighing shall flee away; Man

The Sovereignty of God

shall stand glorified in the Presence of God, and shall be made like Him, seeing Him as He is;—and God, the Sovereign of all orders of beings, the King Eternal, the Only Wise, the Only Infinite, of Whom are all things, by Whom are all things, to Whom are all things,—God shall be all in all.

IX

THE APPLICATION OF THE SACRIFICE OF CHRIST TO THE PRESENT CONDITION OF SOCIETY

Let your manner of life be worthy of the Gospel of Christ. In lowliness of mind each counting the other better than himself; not looking each of you to his own things, but each of you also to the things of others. Have this mind in you which was also in Christ Jesus.
EPISTLE TO THE PHILIPPIANS.

Bear ye one another's burdens, and so fulfil the law of Christ.   EPISTLE TO THE GALATIANS.

Herein is love, not that we loved God, but that He loved us, and sent His Son to be the Propitiation for our sins. Beloved, if God so loved us, we also ought to love one another.
FIRST EPISTLE OF ST. JOHN.

Hereby know we love, because He laid down His Life for us: and we ought to lay down our lives for the brethren. But whoso hath the world's goods, and beholdeth his brother in need, and shutteth up his compassion from him, how doth the love of God abide in him?
FIRST EPISTLE OF ST. JOHN.

The grace of God hath appeared, bringing salvation to all men, instructing us, to the intent that, denying ungodliness and worldly lusts, we should live soberly and righteously and godly in this present world; looking for the blessed hope and appearing of the glory of our great God and Saviour Jesus Christ, Who gave Himself for us.   EPISTLE TO TITUS.

And Jesus came to them and spake unto them, saying, All authority hath been given unto Me in heaven and on earth. Go ye, therefore, and make disciples of all the nations, baptizing them into the name of the Father, and of the Son, and of the Holy Ghost; teaching them to observe all things whatsoever I commanded you: and lo, I am with you alway, even unto the end of the world.
GOSPEL OF ST. MATTHEW.

Chapter IX

The Application of the Sacrifice of Christ to the Present Condition of Society

WHEN we entered upon our present course of thought, we defined Christianity as the Gospel of the Divine Sacrifice. We said: Christianity derives its name from Christ, its meaning from the Cross. Christianity reduced to its simplest terms, gives "Jesus Christ and Him crucified." One purpose has run through these chapters: to unfold a doctrine of God consistent with Jesus Christ and Him crucified, to see God in the light of His supreme Self-revelation as the crucified Saviour of mankind. It remains to point out some of the ways in which such a Gospel of the Divine Sacrifice as

An Application of Sacrifice

we have described tends to modify our opinions and our conduct as members of human society; in other words, to apply the Sacrifice of Christ to the present condition of society, and to individual personality and conduct.

On general principles, it may be assumed that one's social opinions and conduct are affected by one's beliefs. It is almost an axiom, that as a man thinketh in his heart, so is he. Motives of expediency may induce an individual to affect among men a manner of life not supported by his secret convictions. But such expedients are usually as transparent as they are hazardous. What society is, commonly represents with fairness what society believes. This fact, true in connection with so many of our beliefs, is obviously true in connection with our belief about God. One's doctrine of God determines largely one's doctrine of living.

An Application of Sacrifice

"As He is, so are we in this world;" that is, our conceptions of God, of His attitude toward man, of His purpose for man, of His relation to the trouble and misery of life, strongly influence our views of living and our opinions on many subjects affecting the order and well-being of society. If a man is a fatalist in his belief about God, he is apt to be a fatalist in his opinions about men and in his conduct toward men. Back of the Turkish atrocities lies the Turkish belief,— a fatalistic doctrine of God. The bloody foreground of their social conduct corresponds with the lurid background of their faith, which is fatalism. As God has inexorably determined all things, so that whatever is, is that which was to be; therefore to butcher Armenians is but the Will of God.

As far from fatalism as the west is from the east, is the doctrine of God which has been expanding be-

An Application of Sacrifice

fore us in the Gospel of the Divine Sacrifice. Without attempting to re-state in detail conclusions which are now familiar, a few sentences will bring out the contrasts between conclusions we have reached and those reached by others as earnest and as conscientious as ourselves in their desire to know God. It is held by some that God, by an eternal decree, has fixed in advance the destinies of individuals, appointing some to inevitable salvation, abandoning others to inevitable damnation. But we have seemed to see in the Election Scriptures the possibility of an alternate interpretation; namely, God's eternal Purpose of love for the whole race, that it shall be conformed to the Image of His Son; a purpose whose fulfilment in the individual is conditioned upon the will of the individual who, made by God to possess the power of choice, is not under any circum-

An Application of Sacrifice

stances dehumanized by the Maker through the withdrawal of that individual liberty.

It is held by some that the Atonement is limited, that Christ died for the elect only; but we have seemed to see in His Death a universal reference, a tasting of death for every man, a Propitiation for the whole world.

It is held by some that God's attitude toward man is one of wrath and destructive intent, and that that wrath has been appeased only by the gracious and heroic conduct of Christ, Who has interposed between us and God, to save us, by His Death, from God's anger; but we have seemed to see that the purpose of the Loving Christ is identical, in the Unity of the Godhead, with the purpose of the Loving Father, and that the Atonement is the act of the Godhead, whereby Divine Holiness condemns sin, that Divine Love

An Application of Sacrifice

may forgive sin, and may still fulfil its eternal purpose for the beloved race.

It is held by some that the trouble and miseries of life are in accordance with the mysterious Will of God, and, for some inscrutable reason, are permitted to distress mankind; and that they are steps in the plan of love. But we have seemed to see that all misery is part of the universal blight of sin; that it is not directly or indirectly permitted or consented unto by the Will of God; that it is not His Plan, but is the outcome of man's innumerable and constant misuses of freedom; and that the Sovereignty of God is shown not by the permission of evil foreign to His Nature, nor by licensing the sin which causes evil, but by bringing onward through the ages His glorious Plan of good, and by still carrying it on toward its final consummation through and in spite of all the evils wrought by sin, and

An Application of Sacrifice

without depriving man of his individual right of freedom, however much man may abuse that right, and, by that abuse, hinder the Purpose of his Loving Father.

If, as we have already remarked, a fatalistic doctrine of God tends to fatalistic opinions about life and fatalistic conduct toward men, it is proper to inquire, after having stated these conclusions, at which we have arrived through studying the Gospel of the Divine Sacrifice, how such views of God as these modify our views of living, and affect our attitude toward some of the modern conditions of society. St. Paul, in that Epistle which contains, perhaps, the most magnificent *résumé* ever given of the manner and meaning of the Divine Sacrifice, says: " Let your manner of life be worthy of the Gospel of Christ; in lowliness of mind each counting the other better than himself; not

An Application of Sacrifice

looking each of you to his own things, but each of you also to the things of others. Have this mind in you which was also in Christ Jesus." As those magnificent words come to us we look forth upon the present condition of society, and ask, How does the Gospel of the Divine Sacrifice relate itself to-day to human society? We note three facts which very largely cover the situation: The Present Crisis in Human Society; The Disastrous Effects upon Society of an erroneous doctrine of God; The Hope for Society contained in a true application of the Gospel of the Divine Sacrifice.

a. The Present Crisis in Human Society. It is a large thing to speak of; and yet, if one can sketch in its outlines, one brings it within range. Its outlines are these: the growth of knowledge, the growth of individualism, the growth of irreligion, the weakness of the Church. The growth

An Application of Sacrifice

of knowledge is the great modern miracle. Knowledge is no longer the monopoly of a class. It has become the common possession of the race. The children who live in tenement houses to-day have better advantages than the children in baronial castles three hundred years ago. The laborer, going to his work to-day, may buy for the smallest sum in our coinage what an earl of the fifteenth century could not have purchased with a sack of sovereigns: the contemporary news of the world. There was a time when knowledge was the forbidden fruit, guarded by a jealous caste from indiscriminate depredations of unwashed humanity. We may be on the threshold of a time when the possession of knowledge will be compulsory; when the state may make it a misdemeanor not to know. As the result of the growth of knowledge we find the growth of individualism. When men

An Application of Sacrifice

are in a state of ignorance, they run in droves, like dumb, driven cattle. When they get knowledge, they think for themselves. And the more they think the more they differ; the droves break up, turn, trample their drovers, and scatter into individualism. It is an error to call anarchy the child of ignorance. Anarchy is the child of knowledge, fed on false ideas of God. As the result of the growth of individualism we find the growth of irreligion. "Irreligious" means, "destitute of religion;" "not controlled by religious motives or principles." According to the terms of this definition, there are more irreligious people in our civilization now than ever before. Does individualism necessarily produce irreligion? By no means. If that were true, it would mean that ignorance is the protector of religion. There is no natural reason why growth of knowledge and the

An Application of Sacrifice

corresponding growth of individualistic thought should lead to irreligion. Because people think for themselves, is no reason why they may not think alike about God. Why then do we find the growth of individualism followed by the growth of irreligion? Why do we find in our civilization immense multitudes who, we will not say antagonize religion, but let it alone, have nothing to do with it, live without it, in an individualism of pure godlessness? Because of the weakness of the Church. It is not easy to speak of the weakness of the Church. It is to be feared that Christians tend to exaggerate, in their own minds, the strength of the Church. They see it through the warm light of enthusiasm and affection. In many ways the Church is strong as a factor in human affairs. She has large properties; she has an influential and numerous membership; she has heavy moral weight in

An Application of Sacrifice

the balance of current questions: and yet over the individuals who, by the million, make up society, the influence of the Church in this age of universal knowledge and independent thought is not what it was in an earlier age of greater ignorance and lesser liberty. In that earlier age, the Church had a temporal power over the bodies and properties of men which she has long since surrendered to the growing forces of constitutional government. So also in that twilight age of popular ignorance, the Church could appeal to men through their superstitious fears, and could hold them by her mystical threatenings in ways that have largely vanished, and are destined utterly to vanish in the broad, unromantic daylight of common knowledge. While losing these artificial aids, characteristic of less intelligent times, it does not appear that the Church has evolved any new principle of leadership suffi-

An Application of Sacrifice

ciently powerful to draw the multitude in this great modern age of individualism. It does not seem as if she had enough to give men, to keep pace with the new deeds of human society developed under the new conditions of advanced knowledge and entire liberty of thought. Therefore we behold with the growth of individualism, the growth of irreligion ; the decline of popular interest in the Lord's Day, the widespread disposition to substitute for communion with God secular humanitarianism; and the culture of the social instincts for holiness, and the life of faith. This, briefly sketched in outline, appears to be the Present Crisis in Human Society. It has been long and slowly coming, as growing knowledge has brought growing individualism, and growing individualism has, through the weakness of the Church, scattered to some extent the material of society in growing irre-

An Application of Sacrifice

ligion. This crisis is now upon us. For the last ten or twenty years Christians have slowly been waking up to it. To-day they are awake. Awake to two facts: on the one hand, the disastrous effects upon society of a mistaken doctrine of God; on the other hand, the hope for society contained in a true application of the Gospel of the Divine Sacrifice.

b. It has already been said that growing irreligion is not a necessary result of growing knowledge. It cannot be that He Who is the Source of all knowledge has made man so that knowledge pulls him away from God. It cannot be that He Who redeemed Humanity by a Divine Sacrifice and has established His Church in the earth for a witness to His Sacrifice, has built that Church on lines so narrow that society outgrows the Church by ceasing to be ignorant and super-

An Application of Sacrifice

stitious, and by becoming intelligent and free to think for itself. This supposition is incredible. It can be raised only to be dismissed. But another question rises in its stead that cannot be waived aside. Has the Church weakened herself by teaching a doctrine of God, and a doctrine of the Church, and a doctrine of humanity which, however conscientiously taught, has failed to express the deepest meaning of that Gospel which Christ delivered to the world? Has the Church built up a theory of God which has made it hard for humanity to fling itself, with all its sin and sorrow, upon the Heart of God? Has the Church made God seem to be other than He is — an angry Sovereign, damning unborn generations for uncommitted sins; a vindictive Judge, seizing the innocent Christ and slaying Him for the guilty; a pitiless oppressor, beating a helpless race with the nine-

An Application of Sacrifice

tailed whip of misery, sorrow, accident, disease, poverty, overwork, death? As the conditions of human society change, as superstition melts away before the growth of knowledge, as constitutional liberty strikes off the fetters from human thought, it is possible that the traditional doctrine of God, by failing to express the fulness of the Gospel, may have had something to do with that popular cry of to-day that the old Church teachings are outgrown by men of thought. If that cry could only be modified in one single particular, possibly it would state a truth. The Unitarians are right in their "forward movement," as far as it goes; right in saying that the thought of men appears to be growing away from some of the old Church teaching, and to be approaching the point where Christian religion shall be understood to be an expression on

An Application of Sacrifice

earth of the spirit of Jesus Christ. Can they not go one step farther? Can they not advance to the supernaturalism of the New Testament? Can they not acknowledge Who Jesus Christ is, according to the New Testament, and admit that Christianity is the expression on earth of the Gospel of the Divine Sacrifice, God giving Himself on earth in love for man? The best thought of the world has not outgrown the New Testament. The best thought of the world is growing toward the New Testament, and toward the magnificent proportions of that doctrine of God which is announced to the world in the Gospel of the Divine Sacrifice.

c. If it be true that an erroneous doctrine of God is a vital disaster to society, then one is justified in saying that the hope for society, under its present conditions, would be contained in a true application to those

An Application of Sacrifice

conditions of the Gospel of the Divine Sacrifice. The hope that is bound up for mankind with a widening appreciation of God as He is revealed in the Atonement, is the most blessed theme of which a man can speak. We stand at a point in the history of religious thought when, like the light of the sunrise touching peak after peak of the mountains or glorifying league after league of the sea, there is spreading from mind to mind a new conception of that ancient Gospel—God is Love. The old earth-born gloomy cloud is passing away from between man and the Face of God. The lurid scholastic legends of Divine anger and revenge and destructive intent are fading from the minds of men; and suffering humanity, lifting up its eyes in earthly torment, is beginning to discern the light of the knowledge of the glory of God in the Face of Jesus Christ.

An Application of Sacrifice

And our religion is beginning to recover the primitive New Testament conception of the Atonement, as God's sorrowing act of Self-humiliation, inspired by His immortal love for us men, His immortal desire for our salvation; and we are beginning to believe that what Humanity most needs is that revelation of the Love of God, that inspiration to a better life, that consolation in trouble, and that tender, redemptive help in weakness and temptation and failure which were revealed once for all in the Gospel of the Divine Sacrifice. The words of St. John are coming back to the best thought of men, in these last days, like a long lost chord of music: "Herein is love, not that we loved God, but that He loved us, and sent His Son to be the Propitiation for our sins. Beloved, if God so loved us, we also ought to love one another." It is the beginning of a

An Application of Sacrifice

new era, and if its consummation be not suddenly hastened by the glorious appearing of our Great God and Saviour, Jesus Christ, we shall see this new spirit of love giving back to the Church all the influence over human thought she seemed to be losing when, with the growth of knowledge, men seemed to be outgrowing faith. Men cannot outgrow faith, if that faith be founded in a true doctrine of God. The growth of knowledge only broadens those faculties by which we know the value of truth, and the best thought of men ever grows toward, not away from, a true doctrine of God, for man intuitively feels and confesses his need of God. And if this true doctrine of God can be set forth before human society in all its height and depth and length and breadth, if God can at length be shown to men as He is, the Friend and Lover of all souls, Who came

An Application of Sacrifice

of His own free will into this world to seek and to save, Who has tasted death "for us men and for our salvation," Who suffers with man in all his sorrows and needs, and Who is working out for man a glorious destiny in which the strongest and the weakest alike may share, we shall see, and even now are we beginning to see, how Jesus Christ and Him crucified may alter the opinions and the conduct of men in the twentieth century. Changes that are now only in their slow beginning will mature; opinions that are now held only by a few will strengthen into general convictions; In the treatment of criminals, in the growth of social tenderness, in the progress of Catholic Unity, and in the zeal for missions, the prediction is here ventured that we shall see the Gospel of the Divine Sacrifice applied more and more practically to the existing conditions of society.

An Application of Sacrifice

The treatment of criminals shall be considered in the light of the Divine Sacrifice. The chief end of judicial action toward wrongdoers will be seen, in the light of a larger doctrine of God, to be redemptive; and though the safety of society may require in specific instances the lifelong separation of the offender, no crime will be thought to justify the punishment of death. The gallows and the electric chair have no place in an advanced Christian civilization. They are survivals of a mode of thought and of a mode of conduct which characterized an earlier age. The killing of men, on the evidence and judgment of men who are themselves to die, grows out of a mistaken idea that death is an act of God, and that under certain circumstances we have a right to forestall that act and to precipitate that judgment. But we shall reach the time when even our courts shall recog-

An Application of Sacrifice

nize that the conditions which lead up to murder have oftenest their essential causes far back of the individual guilty of the crime; and society will at length admit that He Who tasted death for every man can love even a murderer, and can have a plan of grace for him with which sinful and fallible men have no right to tamper.

Day by day we all feel that a new spirit of social sympathy is springing up among men. Its true cause is the better understanding of the Gospel of the Divine Sacrifice. All who study attentively the signs of the times, must note (with Mr. Benjamin Kidd)[1] the new spirit of tenderness that is spreading through the most prosperous class in the social order toward those who have less opportunity in the struggle of life. And, as he points out, religion is its root; the religion of love constrain-

[1] Social Evolution, pp. 158-165, ed. 1894, Macmillan.

An Application of Sacrifice

ing to the expression of love. Wondrously is this spirit spreading, wondrously is it destined to spread, as men grow to realize that God looks on human miseries with an infinitely deeper pity than man can feel, and that all that we can do to relieve suffering, to guide and counsel ignorance, to throw light into dark and dreary places, to spend and be spent for others, is along the line of that eternal Plan of the All-Loving One, which human sin and failure may hinder, but cannot wholly turn aside. Yes! It is the long-lost chord of St. John's music coming back: " Hereby know we love, because He laid down His Life for us: and we ought to lay down our lives for the brethren. But whoso hath the world's goods and beholdeth his brother in need, and shutteth up his compassion from him, how doth the love of God abide in him?"

An Application of Sacrifice

Every lover of Catholic Unity must look into the twentieth century with hope, when he perceives how the best thought of Christians is tending more and more to relate the Gospel of the Divine Sacrifice to a unified Church. Christ is being lifted up in these latter days, and light is pouring upon His Cross, as Biblical study insists on breaking from mediæval trammels and going back to claim its liberty in the Scriptures. Far are we now from Catholic Unity. Still does the Church persist in weakening herself by setting arbitrary difficulties in the way of unity, but while official stumbling-blocks abound, the hearts of those who rejoice in Him are drawn near to one another; and as this larger perception of God's Love deepens everywhere, no sudden and great advance toward Catholic Unity could surprise us, nor be larger than we should hope for among those

An Application of Sacrifice

from whose vision of God the clouds of gloomy error have melted away.

The Gospel of the Divine Sacrifice is the essential inspiration of missions. The evangelizing of the world, the making disciples of all the nations, was the primitive idea of Christianity. "All authority," said Christ, "has been given unto Me in heaven and on earth. Go ye therefore and make disciples of all the nations, baptizing them into the name of the Father, and of the Son, and of the Holy Ghost, teaching them to observe all things whatsoever I commanded you. And lo! I am with you alway, even unto the end of the world." For centuries, while the Church seemed to incline toward a fatalistic doctrine of God, the evangelizing of the world languished. For centuries she had practically no missions. But now, in this last century, with its tremendous growth in knowledge and in individualism,

An Application of Sacrifice

with its mighty movement of liberalism, we have witnessed the growth of modern missions, which have spread to every part of the earth, and which were never dearer to Christians than to-day, when fanatical persecutions have risen up against them in foreign lands. Those persecutions seem, both at home and on the mission field, to have had no other effect than that of deepening the conviction that missions must go on, and shall go on, at any cost of money or of blood. Why this glorious earnestness? Why this joyous and heroic unanimity? Because the sweet, clear, simple Gospel of the New Testament is coming back and taking its place in human thought, weary with speculation and dogmatism. The long lost chord is ringing everywhere through Christian hearts: "God is Love! God is Love!!" The world is full of sorrow, full of failure, full of

An Application of Sacrifice

devilish sin and shame, but — God is Love; God is Love! the Saviour of the world, the Friend of the friendless, the Light of Life, the Conqueror of Death!

X

THE NEW TESTAMENT IDEA OF PERSONALITY

For in Him we live and move and have our being.

      ACTS OF THE APOSTLES.

And the God of Peace Himself sanctify you wholly, and may your spirit and soul and body be preserved entire, without blame, at the coming of our Lord Jesus Christ.

   FIRST EPISTLE TO THE THESSALONIANS.

Chapter X

The New Testament Idea of Personality

In his Athenian oration St. Paul asserts Man's life in God. "In Him we live and move and have our being." In one of his Thessalonian letters he declares God's Life in Man: "God Himself sanctify you wholly, and may your spirit and soul and body be preserved entire at the coming of our Lord." By co-ordinating these two thoughts, — Man's life in God, God's Life in Man, — we obtain the New Testament idea of Personality. The most wondrous thing about life, for one who accepts the New Testament Idea of Personality, is life itself. Nothing that man *does* is so wonderful as what man *is*. Here is where a true

New Testament Idea of Personality

plan of living should begin; not at the thought of what one does or plans to do, but, first of all, at the thought of what one *is*. The Idea of Personality should be clear before the idea of conduct can be clear. Before I can intelligently ask myself, "What shall I do?" I ought to ask myself: "Who am I?" "Whence am I?" "What am I?" The lives of many would be calmer, broader, richer, worthier, if they had known themselves better, if they had given deeper thought to Personality as the great fact that precedes conduct; and the whole level of conduct would be raised and dignified if the remembrance of what we *are* were present in what we *do*. Therefore to present the New Testament Idea of Personality is to present thoughts that lie close to daily life; it is not to lead into regions of speculative philosophy far from the questions pressing on us day by day, and from

New Testament Idea of Personality

the practical interests that are demanding our attention. It is directly to help one to answer those urgent life questions and to take hold of those practical interests; it is to make better men and women, better fathers and mothers, better sons and daughters, better husbands and wives, better citizens, better leaders and teachers of others, better and wiser trustees of our own selves. The two texts to which reference was made at the opening of the chapter, are utterances of one and the same person; of the man to whose writings we must look for the fullest expression of the New Testament Idea of Personality. Because both utterances are by the same author, we naturally expect the thought in the one to be confirmed and perhaps expanded by the thought in the other. We find this to be the case. St. Paul's fundamental idea about human personality recognized the threefold nature of man, — body, mind, and spirit; a physical life with its appropriate functions and powers; an intellectual life with its characteristic affections and ambitions; a spiritual life with its direct relationship to the Spirit of God. In the quotation from the Athenian speech we find at least an implied recognition of the threefold nature of man's personality, as a life lived in God: "In Him we live and move and have our being." Viewed in the light of his other sayings on the same subject, this threefold expression seems to indicate his belief that each realm of our threefold personality, — the bodily life, the mental life, the spirit life, — is related to God, and continues to exist because of its relation to God. And on the other hand, as to God's Life in Man, his belief is that God may act directly in each realm of man's threefold personality, for the purpose of making the

New Testament Idea of Personality

whole man holy, and of preserving the *whole* man intact for the enjoyment of a splendid destiny. " May God sanctify you wholly, and preserve entire your spirit and soul and body at the coming of the Lord." This is God's Life in Man according to the New Testament, and as such the writer presents it now, with its corresponding truth of Man's life in God, — as one of the conclusions issuing from the Gospel of the Divine Sacrifice. It appears necessary not only that one shall apprehend what is the New Testament Idea of Personality, but that one shall build upon it a distinct conception of conduct and destiny. To promote this result is the writer's objective point. He is not debating the truth or the error of the New Testament Idea of Personality. He is not engaging in controversy with others who may have promulgated ideas of personality which depart from the teachings of the New Tes-

New Testament Idea of Personality

tament. He is engaged purely and simply in an attempt to report what the New Testament Idea is, and in urging the acceptance of that idea as a working hypothesis in one's own thought about one's self. A man must think about himself, or live a shallow, vacillating life; he must have a theory of who he is, and what he is, and whence he is, or be in his conduct like the senseless weather-vane, blown this way and that way by any wind of passion, prejudice, or pugnacity that happens to be blowing; he must have some settled basis of self-knowledge on which to stand and from which to administer the affairs of daily life, or be like a bit of wreckage on the sea of time, tossed to and fro, and stranded at last by the fury of some wave higher than the rest.

When one reflects that life is hurrying through its earthly experience, leaving days, months, and years behind as in the foaming

New Testament Idea of Personality

wake of some mighty steamship; when one considers what man's temptations are and what they may yet be; when one recalls what helplessness to resist evil, and what sad and sweeping defeat have marked and closed the careers of some who have lived without any settled and established sense of their own personality in its relation to God, — well may there arise a longing that cannot be uttered, to make clear to others the bearing upon themselves of Man's life in God and God's Life in Man.

"For in Him we live and move and have our being." Such, according to the New Testament, is Man's life in its relation to God. "In Him we live;" that is to say, as St. Paul declares in the same speech: "He is not far from every one of us, and we are His offspring." In Him we live. Whatever life is, — and no one has yet

New Testament Idea of Personality

been able to say just *what* life is,— all the biological laboratories in all the universities of the world have not been able to discover what life is,— but *whatever* it is, life is something given, not self-derived. Life comes from life; life comes not without pre-existing life. We know that we live, although we cannot say what life is. And the New Testament Idea of life is that in his life man touches that Great Life outside himself Which was, and is, and is to be from all eternity unto all eternity. *In* Him we live; in Him every part of us lives,— body, mind, spirit. Let this thought take hold of the mind for a moment. See to what conclusions it leads; see what divineness it brings into manhood, into womanhood; see with what sacredness it clothes personality, until instead of living with only a few distant and formal thoughts about God, thoughts which really

New Testament Idea of Personality

have had little bearing on anything done or planned, one finds the thought of God brought into everything, and the most ordinary and familiar duties, acts, and relations of life suddenly set forth in a new and grander light.

"In Him we live and move and have our being." Man has a living body, fearfully and wonderfully made; an organism of incalculable intricacy and delicacy, wondrous in its powers, amazing in its uses; a physical creation, which yet is the vehicle and organ of all intellectual and spiritual expression. To think of life, even of the bodily life, as in some true and most mysterious way an outcome and result of the Life of the Infinite God, brings the glory of the Divine even into the realm of the physical. As Christ, the Eternal and Uncreated Son, the Word That was before all worlds, came into manhood's world, and

New Testament Idea of Personality

dwelt in a body, making it and all manhood forever a consecrated thing; so we bring even into our physical life this august and infinite idea of God's Life as the cause of our own, and behold, personality, even according to the flesh, becomes in our thought sacred and honorable and close to God.

Man has a thinking mind, an emotional nature; imagination, memory, powers of intellectual expression. Thought is a form of life. The functions of the body no more reveal life than do the energies of the mind. Ah! how intensely at times we feel the throb and rush of the mind's life, when we have reached some hour of over-mastering recollection, in the pain of which the mind quivers like a suffering animal; or some hour of eager reasoning, in the gladness of which the mind soars and poises and darts onward like an untamed eagle! Yes, thought

New Testament Idea of Personality

is life, — suffering or seraphic life. And whence and what is this life of the mind? Where did this most marvellous form of vitality find its origin? How shall we account for our power to think? The New Testament answers: "In Him we live and move and have our being." *In Him* — not far, not far from every one of us. Ah! it is wonderful. When I think, — even when I think unworthily, — I am using a power that sprang out of God. Thought is the offspring of God.

Man has a spirit: a part of personality that responds directly to God; and, if it has life in it, goes forth in love to God, desires Him, seeks after Him, continually offers itself up to Him in the yearning for holiness. In many the spirit is dead because of sin; it lies unconscious within the life; its characteristic functions are not found; there is no reaching out for God, no communion with Him, no longing to be like Him: the spirit within the man, the woman, is paralyzed; its activities are suspended; it is death in life. But in others there is spiritual response; will and purpose are going forth toward the Living God. How came that spirit to live? By what power was it brought out of death into life? Who made it able to desire God, to love God, to imitate God? The New Testament answers: "In Him we live and move and have our being." Yes, the movement of the human spirit is life, life taken directly from contact with God's Life, as one lights a candle from the flame of the altar. " The spirit of man is the candle of the Lord."

We have spoken of Man's life in God; his whole being touching God at every moment and at every point; and all human life, its spiritual energy, its mental force, its bodily

New Testament Idea of Personality

potency, an outcome and an effect of Divine Power.

But the New Testament Idea of Personality goes farther, and speaks of God's Life in us. We are not only living in Him insomuch that every part of our life depends upon Him, but He is living in us with a great purpose to make every part of our life worthy of Himself now, and worthy of its splendid destiny hereafter. " The God of peace Himself sanctify you wholly, and may your spirit and soul and body be preserved entire and without blame at the coming of our Lord Jesus Christ." To speak of God's Life in us is to speak of God's Purpose and Will for our personality. And what is His Will for us? What would He do in us? He would sanctify us wholly, and preserve our body, mind, and spirit entire and without blame at the coming of our Lord Jesus Christ.

New Testament Idea of Personality

It has already been pointed out that the idea of personality should be clear before the idea of conduct *can* be clear; that before we can intelligently ask "What shall I do?" we ought to ask "Who am I?" and "What am I?" for what we do must be determined largely by what we are. The great determining question of conduct should of course be: "Lord, what wilt Thou have me to do?" but before one can ask that question with full intelligence he should ask another, which may be called the great determining question of personality: "Lord, what wouldst Thou do in me?" Let us be sure that we know what God's Life in us is seeking to accomplish, and then shall we realize the greatness of our personality in God's sight and be the more anxious to put our personality entirely into His hands and to do whatever He would have us to do. So we ask: "Lord, what wouldst Thou do in me?" and He answers: "Sanctify thee wholly, and preserve thy body and mind and spirit entire and without blame at the Lord's coming." Not till we have realized all this do we know how great our personality is. God would sanctify and preserve our *bodily life*. These physical lives of ours mean much to Him. The profanation and misuse of them is horrible in His sight. The reverent and stainless maintenance of them is that to which He seeks to lead us by dwelling in us. To Him the body is a Temple, not of the human spirit alone, but of the Holy Spirit, the Divine Spirit, God Himself, and He would have us regard this part of our personality as holy in His sight and in our own. This is one great message of the Incarnation to such as will receive it: the Word made flesh glorified the flesh, so that whosoever profanes it profanes the Substance of Christ's Person.

New Testament Idea of Personality

God would sanctify and preserve our *minds*. From the miserable incubus of intellectual indolence, from the ruthless squandering of time on vain and vapid fancies, from the poisonous breath of unhallowed imaginations, from the petrifying influence of selfishness, from the weakness of pride and vanity, from the deadly passions of hatred and jealousy, from everything that can impoverish mental strength, — God would sanctify and preserve our minds. God lives in us to make our mental life beautiful, to kindle by His mysterious Life-touch perceptions of all greatness and loftiness of thinking, to anoint with wisdom the eyes of our understanding, that they may see and choose the best in all things.

God would sanctify and preserve our *spirits*. His Life is in us to make for holiness. The power of His Spirit bears on us to make us like unto Himself. He who made us

New Testament Idea of Personality

regenerate, having begotten us again unto a living hope through the power of Christ's Resurrection, would now educate and expand these spirits of ours by the constant discipline of grace, that we may be worthy of the calling with which we are called, and may be as light-bearers in the world, holding forth the word of life.

Such appears to be the New Testamemt Idea of Personality; Man's life in God: "In Him we live and move and have our being;" God's Life in Man, seeking to sanctify him wholly, and to preserve entire and blameless, for an immortal destiny, the threefold life, — body, mind, and spirit.

As we hold up before us this great Biblical conception of personality, a conception so broad, so comprehensive, so full of dignity and affectionateness, so perfectly in accord with one's highest ideal of what must be the Will of God for man, light falls from this theme upon the three great thoughts which in our minds lie nearest to personality: the thought of sin, the thought of redemption, the thought of destiny.

Light falls upon the thought of sin as a discordant and abnormal fact that has intruded itself into our personality; light that reveals sin in all its true horror as a grief to God and an offence against our truest life. Sin is every choice we make for ourselves, every thought we think, every word we speak, every deed we do against the normal conditions of our own personality. We have seen what those normal conditions are, how full of splendor, hope, and opportunity — our life in God, God's Life in us. Every sin is a wounding of God's Life in us, a grieving of the Holy Spirit, an affront to Him Who is within us, because of His mighty love for us. Every sin is a blow dealt at one's

New Testament Idea of Personality

own personality, — an act of lawlessness, a setback to character, a defiling and defamation of this most holy treasure of our life.

And again, as we hold up this great New Testament conception of personality, *light falls from it upon the thought of Redemption*, and we are brought to co-ordinate the Redemption of man with the Creation of man, and to see that what was created was also redeemed. What was created was personality, — the threefold unity, — body, mind, spirit. What was redeemed was personality — the three-fold unity — body, mind, spirit. Can any one think this thought out to its conclusions and not be thrilled with a deeper sense of the sanctity of life? Has Christ indeed suffered for my spirit in the anguish of His Spirit? Has Christ indeed redeemed my mind in the loneliness and humiliation of His own? Has

New Testament Idea of Personality

Christ indeed bathed my body in the Mystic Stream that burst from His smitten Heart? Oh, wonder of wonders! to be not only a person living in God and lived in by God, but to be a redeemed person, every part of whom, one's physical being, one's mental being, one's spiritual being, has been taken by Christ, in His own Person, up to the altar of pain and death, and there consecrated unto newness of life!

And finally, when we hold up this great New Testament Idea of Personality, *light falls from it upon the thought of Destiny.* What is to be the Destiny of the redeemed personality, when the Will of God concerning it shall all be accomplished? It is all so precious to us, in the persons of those whom we have perfectly known and perfectly loved. Body, mind, spirit; these, in our dearest, are but one in our thought; we cannot separate them. But are

New Testament Idea of Personality

they to be separated in their destiny? Is death the eternal rending of personality? Does the grave swallow up forever that precious part of personality which it receives? Is there no giving back? Is there no resurrection in glory of that which was glorious in God's sight once, and in ours; that which He sanctified and we loved? Let them who will, believe that the body has no destiny beyond the intense and abhorrent humiliation of the awful grave; but as for me, may my tongue cleave to the roof of my mouth, and my right hand forget her cunning in the day when I cease to believe that He Who redeemed and sanctified the whole personality — body, mind, and spirit — shall at last recover and reconstruct in immortal completeness that which was rent asunder in Death's Catastrophe. By every grave of one of Christ's own, still shall I stand, seeing by anticipation there, His own

New Testament Idea of Personality

Grave emptied in Resurrection; by every friend sleeping the last mysterious sleep, still shall I dare to say that great evangelical prophecy of a reconstructed personality: "For this corruptible must put on incorruption, and this mortal must put on immortality; so when this corruptible shall have put on incorruption, and this mortal shall have put on immortality, then shall be brought to pass the saying that was written: Death is swallowed up in victory." What then is the message to the individual of this New Testament Idea of Personality? It is this. To live day by day as one whose whole personality — body, mind, and spirit — is knit to the very Life of God; to live as one whose whole personality — body, mind, and spirit — is being lived in by the Eternal Sanctifier, seeking to make one worthy to be the living, breathing shrine of God; to live as one whose whole person-

New Testament Idea of Personality

ality — body, mind, and spirit — is redeemed in Christ for an immortal destiny, indestructible by Death, to be preserved entire in the hand of the All-Loving Keeper, and to be presented blameless, joyous, and complete at last, at the Coming of our Lord Jesus Christ.

XI

CONDUCT; OR, THE CROWNING
OF ONESELF

Whether therefore ye eat or drink, or whatsoever ye do, do all to the glory of God.

    First Epistle to the Corinthians.

Hold that fast which thou hast, that no man take thy crown.

    The Revelation of St. John.

Chapter XI

Conduct; or, The Crowning of Oneself

A SCENE of extraordinary splendor was the coronation of the Czar of Russia at Moscow. Possibly in all modern history there has not been any great function of state more superbly conceived and executed in its material detail. Sailors climbed the aerial pinnacles of palace-like Churches and wove electric lights about them in the meshes of a glittering web. The representatives of all terrestrial empires, attended with suites sumptuously apparelled, came travelling from the north, the south, the east, the west, converging on Moscow like the rays of a sunburst. The strong rooms of the Romanoffs were unlocked, and

Conduct; the Crowning of Oneself

poured forth a dazzling stream of gems: pear-shaped rubies, historic diamonds, aquamarines beyond price. Cloths of silver, mantles of ermine and minever, velvets seeded with pearls, jewelled orders, imperial ribbands, troopings of priests and prelates from afar, chantings of seraphic voices, chimings from innumerable bells, thunderings from deep-throated guns, — such was the coronation of the Czar: as a material exhibit of sight and sound, the most that man can do! Yet the material opulence of the occasion was not the most impressive feature of the coronation. Far above all that surrounded it, towered the moral and political significance of a single moment and a single act. The moment and the act were these — when the Czar crowned himself. He crowned himself. Standing beneath the baldachin of the Cathedral, and receiving the crown from the repre-

Conduct; the Crowning of Oneself

sentative of his religion, he suffered no fellow-mortal to set that crown upon him; but, lifting it above himself, with his own hands he placed it firmly on his own head. The Czar crowned himself; and in that single and supreme circumstance lay the significance for good or ill, to Russia and to the world, of the coronation of Nicholas. He declared himself an autocrat, self-consecrated under God; taking the symbol of his life sovereignty, as it were the direct bestowal of God, and appropriating it, without human mediation or intervention, directly to himself. As his figure flashes forth for the moment before the world, the figure of a man putting a crown upon his own head as the sign by which he claims and appropriates a right of living, it gives the suggestion of a thought that bears nobly and truly on each one of us. We may forget the Czar, the auto-

Conduct; the Crowning of Oneself

crat, the courtly surroundings, the ruling over states, and see only a man, standing erect before God, taking a God-given Crown, and putting it with his own hands on his own head. We may see only this: the Crowning of Oneself. And seeing this, we will see the true worth, the real royalty of our own life; we will see why St. John the Divine, — standing in no cathedral made with hands, but standing out under the baldachin of the Grecian skies on the Lord's day morning long ago, and realizing that He on Whose Head are many crowns meant our life to have its self-coronation for service, — should have cried out in his joy and wonder: "Unto Him That loved us, and washed us from our sins in His own Blood, and hath made us kings and priests unto God and His Father, to Him be glory and dominion forever and ever. Amen."

Conduct; the Crowning of Oneself

The Crowning of Oneself. Let us think of it and speak of it. It will be remembered that in the preceding chapter we considered one of the conclusions which appear to issue from the Gospel of the Divine Sacrifice, namely, the New Testament Idea of Personality; Man's life in God — God's Life in Man. Man's whole life, body, mind, and spirit was regarded as subsisting in, and directly related to, God's Life, so that in Him we live and move and have our being; and God's Life was seen to be moving in the whole life of man with a purpose to sanctify it wholly, and to preserve entire and without blame, spirit and soul and body at the Coming of our Lord Jesus Christ. Such was found to be the New Testament Idea of Personality; our life lived in the enfolding atmosphere of the Life of God, and God's Life working with love's noblest Purpose in view in each realm of

Conduct; the Crowning of Oneself

this threefold life of ours. Conduct, considered as the crowning of oneself, is the supplement and completing of the thought of personality. It is important to establish in one's mind a sense of correlation between the two subjects, Personality and Conduct, because they are related, not arbitrarily, but organically and of necessity. Conduct is the crowning of personality. Personality is *being*, Conduct is *doing;* which is the coronation of being with the very glory of God. " Whether therefore ye eat or drink, or whatsoever ye do, do all to the glory of God." What we *do* is the coronation of what we *are*. God has given us our personality, — a thrice noble, thrice holy thing; a thing which lives in all its parts, and moves and has its being in Himself; a thing in which through all its several parts His Life Power seeks to enter and to act unto the sanctifying of the whole being. Yes! God has

Conduct; the Crowning of Oneself

given us our personality, and God, in the Divine Sacrifice, has redeemed personality. Now, what will we do *with* it as thus redeemed, and what will we do *by* it? Wherewithal shall we crown our being for its work and influence in life? Stooping down to that which is beneath us, shall we pick out of the dust, out of the clay of life, the stained and withering garland of sin's pleasure, and put *that* upon brows that were meant for better things — or, standing erect, and conscious of our redemption, before the Face of our Father, shall we receive from His Hand the royal thought of living only unto His Glory, in body, mind, and spirit, and shall we crown ourselves with that thought? Wherewithal shall a redeemed person be crowned for his life work on earth, — with the thorny crown of self-indulgence, that makes a mockery of our personality, or with the glory-

Conduct; the Crowning of Oneself

thought of doing only that which is worthy of one who lives in God — in whom God lives.

The *crowning* of oneself! What an almost terrifying thought is this, that we *must* crown ourselves on earth, by conduct; that conduct is the coronation of personality with the wreath of dishonor or with the circlet of nobleness; and that conduct is what *we* do and what no other can do for us! If in some way it could be done for us; if other hands, wiser, gentler, holier hands than ours could come and set upon our brow the sign that designates us for our place in life and our influence in the world; if one could only *be* without doing! If one could but abide in the calm, high thought of what we *are*, redeemed in Christ's Blood, embraced by the Life of God, and born into this world, each to be a habitation of God through the Spirit; if one could gloriously sub-

Conduct; the Crowning of Oneself

sist in the ideal; dwell always on the high Transfiguration Mount of that superb thought, Man's life in God, God's Life in Man; if the doing of deeds were not always pressing upon us, resolving the ideal into the real, the magnificent abstract into the plain and definite concrete, calling us down from the transfigured mount into the difficult, crowded, perilous, exhausting plain of acts and words! Vainest of dreams! There is no being without doing,—personality without conduct is unthinkable. And there is no doing for us except what we do in ourselves. Conduct is whatsoever we do,—everything in every hour of days and weeks and months and years,—whether we eat or drink or whatsoever we do. Conduct is what we claim for ourselves; the sign we set upon our own brows that shows where we stand and what we declare ourselves to be; and it is a thought

Conduct; the Crowning of Oneself

which might well appall one who is no coward, that some crown, picked from the dust beneath us or taken in reverence from the Hand above us, we must set on our own heads.

But our danger is also our dignity. Drawn down by temptation, one may stoop and pick from the dust the crown of shame and sorrow and self-mockery, and degrade therewith the brow of Personality. That is man's danger, that he *can* do that which is far beneath him, that he can mock himself, and demean himself by conduct unworthy of his high calling in Christ Jesus; but in that possibility which springs from the very construction of his will is also the dignity of a Child of God redeemed in Christ and walking in the Spirit: that he can conceive of conduct as the crown of glory wherewith one may crown oneself; that he has the power to take, from God's offering Hand, an idea of conduct great enough to

Conduct; the Crowning of Oneself

comprehend all life, to declare the royal dignity of all that one does, to set the Kingly Mark on everything, from the greatest to the least item of our daily round. It is with intense enthusiasm, with indescribable interest, one who believes this seeks to set forth before the eyes of others such a thought;—conduct, the *crowning* of personality; a *doing* that is worthy of this *being*; a doing that springs from the remembrance of what one is, and that sets upon the outward life the sign and affirmation of its own value in the sight of God. The crown does not make the king,—the crown set nobly on the head is but the affirmation of the kingship that *is*. What we do does not make us what we are. What we do declares what we are. In every phase of action, in the whole territory of conduct, it is intended that doing shall disclose and affirm the quality of being.

Conduct; the Crowning of Oneself

"Whether therefore ye eat or drink, or whatsoever ye do, *do all* to the glory of God." But we cannot understand how "eating and drinking," and the great multifarious "whatsoever" of life, can be to the glory of God. No, we cannot understand it when we think only of the acts themselves; considered thus, many of them are most undivine, most material, most unimportant acts. But the acts must be thought of in relation to the person who does them. Conduct acquires its meaning and its worth from personality. The significance of the coronation of Nicholas is not in the golden crown considered as an object by itself; it is in the crown considered in relation to the person on whose head it is placed. It is because the Czar *is* the Czar that the crowning of himself becomes an act of royal significance. It is because *we* are what we are that

Conduct; the Crowning of Oneself

conduct means so much. Think of yourself, remember who you are; think of your life in God. and God's Life in you; think what has been God's Purpose for you always, even from out of the eternal past, when, in the glorious thought of His own Mind, He knew His own Intention and Desire concerning this wondrous human personality that was to be in His own Image, knew what He would have man to be; think thoughts like these about yourself if you would know the significance of conduct as the coronation of personality; if you would know how every act — whether we eat or drink or whatsoever we do — *may* be to the glory of God.

And, that you have the right to think such thoughts about yourself — nay, that you are *bound* to think such thoughts about yourself — is plain to him who, believing absolutely the New Testament Idea

Conduct; the Crowning of Oneself

of personality, will take that same blessed New Testament in his hand and will permit the Spirit of God, testifying in the Word, to reason out for him the New Testament logic of conduct as the self-crowning of personality. It then appears that to make "whatsoever we do" to be unto the glory of God does not mean to drag into conduct an unreal and artificial element of sanctity, which must inevitably load one's life with insincere ceremonialism; it means to remember what God the Father in His eternal Purpose desires one to be; it means to remember what God the Son by His work of Redemption makes one to be; it means to remember what God the Spirit, by His indwelling, authorizes one to be.

It means, to remember what God the Father in His eternal Purpose desires one to be. Here is where foreordination finds its place in our

Conduct; the Crowning of Oneself

thinking; not as a grievous yoke of fatalism, but as a perfect law of liberty. New Testament foreordination is not necessarily to be regarded as the fixing of destiny by a decree; it is also possible to regard it as the Purpose, the Desire, the Intention in God's Mind for the personality He has made in His own Image, — God's prophetic coronation of our lives, as lives which are united to His own; that, in time, we, becoming conscious of His Purpose for us, may choose to crown ourselves by conduct worthy of the calling with which we are called, worthy of the royal inheritance our Father has bestowed. "In Him" says St. Paul, "we were made a heritage, having been foreordained according to the Purpose of Him Who worketh all things after the counsel of His Will, that we should be unto the praise of His Glory, we who had before trusted in Christ."

Conduct; the Crowning of Oneself

And then, it is to remember what God the Son, by his work of Redemption, *makes* one to be. "To Him That loved us, and washed us from our sins in His own Blood, and hath made us kings and priests unto God and His Father, to Him be glory forever. For ye are an elect race, a royal priesthood, a holy nation, a people for God's own possession, that ye may show forth the excellencies of Him who called you out of darkness into His marvellous light."

And yet again, it is to remember what God the Spirit, by His Indwelling, authorizes one to be. "Know ye not that your body is the Temple of the Holy Ghost, Which is in you, Which ye have of God; and ye are not your own, for ye are bought with a price; therefore glorify God in your body and in your spirit, which are God's."

Such are the thoughts we have

Conduct; the Crowning of Oneself

the right to think about ourselves,— such the thoughts we are bound to think about ourselves if we hold the New Testament Idea of Personality. And thinking those thoughts, life recovers its dignity and conduct, in the greatest matters and in the smallest; all action, whether we eat or drink, or whatsoever we do, becomes the Crowning of Oneself—the acknowledgment with our own hands and by our own wills of what we are in the Purpose of the Father, in the Love of the Son, in the Grace of the Spirit. This is a glorious doctrine of conduct. It clothes life with new meaning. It sets upon the brow a diadem of self-respect. It makes one stand erect and look upon life as a great privilege to be used, a great trust to be administered. There is nothing in this doctrine of conduct at variance with humility. The publican whom Christ blessed above the Pharisee,

Conduct; the Crowning of Oneself

stood in the Temple and would not so much as lift up his eyes unto heaven, but smote upon his breast and cried, "God be merciful to me a sinner." "Not much," you say, "of the kingly in that attitude" "Not much," you say, "of the crowning of oneself in that smiting of the breast." No, there is not. And that is what sin does. Sin is the unkingly act, sin is the soiling and the bartering of our crown. Sin bows like a bulrush the head that might have been erect, dims with scalding tears of shame eyes that might have looked into the Eyes of God. Sin takes the hands that might have lifted our crown to place it grandly on our brow, and sets them beating sadly and wearily upon our breast. But God would not have only the beating of the breast and the downcast eyes of shame. God loves sinners. God helps the sinful. But sin and the humiliations of sin

Conduct; the Crowning of Oneself

were never our destiny, planned in the Holy Heart of Eternal Love. "He hath chosen us in Him before the foundation of the world, that we should be holy and without blame before Him in love." And if in the self-will of the past we have become unholy, it is no pleasure to God that we should go on beating our breasts forever. If the forgiveness of sins be not a mockery, if the majestic Redemption we commemorate in the Sacrament of the Lord's Body and Blood be not a fiction, there *is* a lifting up of the bowed head possible; there *is* a receiving afresh of the crown and a putting of it on in faith and hope; there is a looking once more with clear eyes into the Face of God, Who, according to His great mercy, has begotten us again unto a living hope by the Resurrection of Jesus from the dead, unto an inheritance incorruptible, undefiled, and that fadeth not away.

Conduct; the Crowning of Oneself

To each life that acknowledges the Purpose of the Father, the Atonement of the Son, the Potency of the Spirit, may it then be said: "Hold that fast which thou hast, that no man take thy crown." Be kingly in your thought and you shall be kingly in your deed. Child of a Royal Father, remember Whose you are and Whom you serve. Kinsman of One erst crowned with thorns, now crowned with many crowns, crown thyself, day by day, by doing *all* unto the glory of God. Let no man take thy crown, thy glorious crown of a *consecrated conduct.* Hold that fast which thou hast; set firmly on thine head, as thy royal right, the belief that whatsoever thou doest has a meaning. and a value in the sight of God, which makes it a glory simply to live one's life. Crown thyself until He crown thee. Fight the good fight. Keep the faith. Finish thy course. Hence-

Conduct; the Crowning of Oneself

forth there is laid up for thee the crown of righteousness, which the Lord, the righteous Judge, shall give thee at that day,—and not to thee only, but to all them that have loved His Appearing.

THE END

www.ingramcontent.com/pod-product-compliance
Lightning Source LLC
Chambersburg PA
CBHW022017240426
43667CB00042B/905